God Chooses People Like You

BEVERLY LIPFORD CARROLL

WESTBOW
PRESS®
A DIVISION OF THOMAS NELSON
& ZONDERVAN

Scripture taken from the Holy Bible, NEW INTERNATIONAL VERSION®. Copyright © 1973, 1978, 1984 by Biblica, Inc. All rights reserved worldwide. Used by permission. NEW INTERNATIONAL VERSION® and NIV® are registered trademarks of Biblica, Inc. Use of either trademark for the offering of goods or services requires the prior written consent of Biblica US, Inc.

WestBow Press books may be ordered through booksellers or by contacting:

WestBow Press
A Division of Thomas Nelson & Zondervan
1663 Liberty Drive
Bloomington, IN 47403
www.westbowpress.com
1 (866) 928-1240

ISBN: 978-1-5127-0840-0 (sc)
ISBN: 978-1-5127-0842-4 (hc)
ISBN: 978-1-5127-0841-7 (e)

Library of Congress Control Number: 2015913177

Print information available on the last page.

WestBow Press rev. date: 09/01/2015

This book is dedicated to the memory of Tena Lustig.
Her loving honesty in life and her unwavering courage in death
reminded all who loved her to never hesitate to trust God.

God Chooses People Like You

Acknowledgements

No significant work, in life or on paper, is done in isolation. I am deeply indebted to so many who have nurtured me during this time:

To the Seekers Sunday School class – You are an incredible blessing God has place on my heart and in my life. I am truly, "eternally" grateful for your presence each week. You allow me to share with you what God has taught me and to hone what God wants me to share with others. Your support allows me to continue to become what God is calling me to be.

To Dr. Roberta Damon – Your wisdom and encouragement have been integral in this project. You have called out the best in me for 28 years. You believed in me, and you helped me believe in myself. You are undoubtedly an "endnote" in the story of my life, just as your insight is woven through the chapters in this book.

To Todd Ball – Your insight helped make what I wrote match what I wanted to say. Thank you for being one whom I can always trust for honesty and support.

To Anne Ball – Perhaps one of God's most precious gifts this side of heaven are those that he gives us as family that we also choose as friends. Your practical wisdom and insight, your kindness and encouragement, your friendship and support, have guided me and given me a safe place to be completely myself and the courage to continue to trust God for what I cannot see.

To my mom, Maureen Lipford – You have always encouraged me to believe in myself and warned me not to let fear of failure limit God's activity in my life. Because of you, I've had the courage to become more of the woman God is calling me to be. I'm so grateful for your love and our friendship…and for your proofreading and grammar expertise!

To Jay, Brad, Brian – How grateful I am that God has given each of you to me. Being your wife and mom are the most important things God has asked me to do. Thank you for your support and patience during the research and writing process, and thank you for the incredible gift of our family. God has blessed me immeasurably through you.

Soli Deo Gloria

Foreword

It's all about choice. The big names of the Bible were not amazing people with remarkable talents; they were ordinary people who chose to trust an amazing God. The Bible is full of instruction about how to make good choices: between right and wrong, between love and hate, between hope and despair, between trust in God and trust in ourselves. Sometimes our choices govern our behavior; sometimes they govern our attitudes. Sometimes we make choices that separate us from God. But sometimes, every once in a "holy" while, our choices to trust and obey him allow us to see his glory and know his presence this side of heaven.

Regardless of our past or our resume, we face the same temptation that Eve did in the garden. Believe what God says, or believe something different. Satan's goal, then and now, is to separate God from his children. He wants to prevent us from bearing fruit because he doesn't want the world to see God's glory in us. His arsenal against us includes all that came as a result of the curse of sin, and his goal is for that arsenal to cripple us, to keep us lost in what can never be, and tied to things that keep us broken. Pride, insecurity, fear, disappointment, betrayal, heartbreak, regret and shame are all tools that Satan hopes to use to destroy us by encouraging us to choose to focus on ourselves, our circumstances, or our enemies.... rather than on our God.

Sometimes we really believe we have good reasons for choosing to ignore or disobey God. Sometimes our disobedience is accidental and without premeditation, but most often it is the result of intentional choices to trust things and people other than God. Some in the Bible were ambushed by uncertainty and difficulties and chose to be victimized by the very thing that Satan used to attack them. But many others heard the unthinkable from God and trusted enough to obey.

Our capabilities are far less influential than the choices we make, and our choices become the stories of our lives. Whom you trust, what you do with your pain and problems will determine whether you will ever know victory in this life, or whether you accept defeat and allow yourself to be defined by those who seek your destruction.

This book will examine some of the events in the Bible where ordinary people like you and me faced a choice: trust and obey God or trust and obey something else. Their struggles and temptations were no different from ours. May we learn from their examples, good and bad, and may we trust God enough to choose to trust his plan, his will, his timing, his power, and his love.

I am awed every day by what my extraordinary God can do. I am brought to my knees every morning in praise and humility. I am overwhelmed when I realize that the Almighty God of the Universe tutors me as I seek his presence and that he uses my Bible and computer to help me find his truth. And I am utterly amazed that he allows someone like me – with all my flaws and my inconsistent obedience, with all the poor decisions of my past and all the complicated issues of my present – to share my journey toward his heart in this book with you. It is my prayer that if you chose to read this book and allow me to share what I've learned with you, that you will be as patient and loving with yourself as God has been with me, that you will find his truth and his presence as you read these pages, and that you will be encouraged to trust him with who you can be, rather than who you have been.

The time I have spent researching and writing and teaching this book have been so precious to me. God has tenderly led me through some deep pain and difficult times as I wrote this book. I can't say that I had amazing new revelations about the character of God during this process, but what I've always known and believed...are more deeply embedded in my heart. Somehow I mean it more now than I used to.

Introduction

The heroes of the Bible weren't any more gifted or powerful than you are. They were flawed, ordinary people, living ordinary lives, doing ordinary things. But they allowed their ordinary lives to be interrupted by God, who is anything but ordinary. They made decisions based on who they knew God to be, rather than on what they knew of their own personal weaknesses. They chose to trust the power of God, rather than the power of their enemy. They chose to obey God when they did not necessarily see a happy ending. And when they did, God's glory shone through them. Only then do they begin to look like super heroes. We see them as amazing people, but what we are looking at is God's reflection in them.

Being extraordinary is not determined by exceptional capability; it is determined by what we choose to do with our ordinary capabilities. Ordinary people are capable of extraordinary things when they seek progress rather than safety, when they refuse to give up even though life is difficult, and when they focus their vision on what can be achieved, rather than what might be disheartening. It took Thomas Edison years to discover exactly how to make the incandescent light bulb. His assessment of that process speaks to his focus and determination. "I have not failed. I've just found 10,000 ways that won't work."[1] The 10,000 ways that did not work did not divert him from the belief that he could harness electricity that would change the world.

I love it that God, not only put the successes of his people in the Bible; he included their failures as well. He was never intimidated by the failure or weakness of his people; God often used their failures and weaknesses to strengthen them for the victory that was to come.

Too many Christians trust God for their salvation, but struggle daily to obey him because they base their choices on themselves, not on God. We are so intimidated by what has happened in the past or what might happen in the future that we refuse to trust the God we cannot control. The chapters of this book will explore some of the reasons we refuse to trust God, for the first time, or ever again. We will examine the stories of people in the Bible who had good reasons to make bad choices. Those choices often cost them the adventure and fullness, joy and peace of a relationship with the Almighty God. Some of the stories are about people who gave their brokenness to God; some stories are about people who were obedient and gave the consequences, whatever they might be, to the God who had proven he was enough.

When I look back at my life, I see major events that mark high and low points. I see repetition of traditions that show the passing of time. I see people and moments that changed the "plot" of my life or changed my perspective. Some moments and events found me at my best; others did not. But all of them comprise my story. Every human who has ever lived has a story.

The stories of the people in the Bible were preserved for us because God knew we would need to learn the same things. But their stories are no more important or precious to the heart of God than yours. He created you for fellowship with him, and he wants to be a part of your story. He wants you to know him (Ps 46:10). He wants more for you than you can imagine for yourself (Eph 3:20). He wants your life to be characterized by abundance and joy (John 10:10 and 17:13).

If that is how God feels about us, then why do we chose to disobey? What happens to us may not be sin, but our response to it can be. When our feelings and expectations become more important than God, we make an idol of them. We allow them the power to control our response. Pride, insecurity, fear, disappointment, betrayal, heartbreak, regret, and shame are not new. The temptations common to people in the Bible are the same ones we face today, and too often we choose to make an idol of our circumstances and disobey God.

When Christians focus on God, rather than their failure, their weakness, or the power of their enemy, the ordinary becomes extraordinary. People in the Bible who chose obedience and trust were able to see the power and glory and presence of God from a front row seat. So can we. But we have to stop pretending to be in charge of things we can't control. In his book *Pursued* Wilhite says "It's time to quit working hard for something that can't be earned."[2] We've got to acknowledge that he is God and we are not. We've got to stop making excuses and start being obedient, even (and especially!) when we can't see the big picture.

1 Cor 1:25 For the foolishness of God is wiser than man's wisdom, and the weakness of God is stronger than man's strength.

We spend so much of our time protecting our ordinariness. We don't want to be interrupted or disobeyed. We want to control our circumstances and have all the details of our lives work out smoothly. We manipulate to implement our own plans and attempt nothing that may cost us security or that requires more than we are capable of accomplishing in our own strength. We don't want to be challenged because we might fail. We don't want to face the truth because the image we have worked so hard to build might shatter. We don't want confrontation because we might be wrong.

I used to excuse my inconsistency and lack of faith because I am not as smart or gifted or strong as the people in the Bible. They got to see and do awesome miracles. They had great adventures where they saw the power of God interrupt history and circumvent natural law. Some of them were allowed to see the physical manifestation of God's presence and actually hear his voice. They had visions and saw angels and witnessed amazing things. Barber echoes this idea in his book.

> "Often we look at the biblical characters of the Old Testament and assume that their obedience was easy and their faith unwavering. We place them on a pedestal and believe that they are somehow closer to God than we could ever hope to be, and we lose our ability to relate with them. Yet, if we look closely and honestly at them we find our own struggles and stumbling mirrored in their lives."[3]

But when I look carefully at the great adventures of the Bible, I realize that all of the awesome revelations and miracles were predicated on situations I would have desperately tried to avoid. Noah's rescue from the flood followed a hundred years of construction that would most certainly have branded him the town kook. David, the teenage shepherd, accepted the challenge of a giant the best warriors in the army of Israel had already refused to fight. Daniel's miraculous rescue required that he spend the night with lions. Mary Magdalen suffered with seven demons before she could know God's deliverance. All the people Jesus healed struggled with physical ailments and hopelessness.

I don't want to be afraid or ridiculed. I don't want to be thrown into a fiery furnace or sold into slavery. I don't want to be falsely accused or put in jail. I don't want to pick up a snake or be swallowed by a fish. I don't want to challenge the authority of someone who has the power to kill me. I don't want to have to defy my government to obey my God. I don't want to mourn or be in pain or suffer or know shame. But it is in situations like those that the obedience of ordinary people shows the extraordinary power of God.

The more I learn about God, the deeper my understanding of his character and his plan, the more I don't want to be separated from him. I am an ordinary woman with real fears and weaknesses who worships a God that has all power and has promised to redeem me, and I want my life to display evidence of the extraordinary God I serve.

God preserved the stories of his people in the Bible so that we can learn from their failures and their triumphs. These stories can warn us, bless us, challenge us, and inspire us. But we must study them. And when we do, we will see that it wasn't the power or giftedness of those people that made them special; it was their relationship with God that made them extraordinary.

God does not require that you pass a test or rise to a particular level of holiness before he will work in you or through you. God does not rely on your self-confidence; he is not deterred by your past, your excuses, your sin, or your shortsighted plans. Moses and David, two of the most powerful men in the Old Testament, and Paul in the New Testament, all committed murder. Jacob was a liar and a cheater. Joseph was a braggart. Noah got drunk. Samson betrayed his vow. Rahab was a prostitute. Peter betrayed Christ. Jesus intentionally chose to hang out with sinners. You have no excuse that is greater than God's ability to redeem and restore.

When people in the Bible chose to obey, God used them and blessed them, regardless of their past or their weaknesses. He offers you the same opportunity.

"In your anger do not sin." (Eph 4:26) There is nothing implicitly wrong with anger, and there is no avoiding it in this life. Anger, like disappointment, regret, shame, heartbreak, insecurity, and betrayal were what happened as a result of man's choice in the garden. Each of those consequences are now part of the story of all who live in this world outside of Eden. What we do with them may or may not become sin, but they are ammunition Satan uses to try to separate us from God. He wants to rob us of God's blessing and keep us enslaved to the consequences of our sin.

The consequences of our weakness and brokenness are inescapable in this fallen world. There is, however, a huge difference between people who live their lives on their own terms and people who trust God. That difference is what they choose to do with their weakness and pain.

We live in a self-focused culture that encourages us to take control of our lives. We are inundated with a myriad of self-help theories in books, on TV, and on the internet. God makes it clear that we are absolutely responsible for our choices, but he also makes it clear that we live in a fallen world and are opposed by Satan himself who "prowls around like a roaring lion, looking for someone to devour". (I Pet 5:8)

Satan's goal is to separate us from God. He doesn't need us to participate in satanic worship ritual to have victory over us; he just needs us to trust something or someone other than God himself. Satan's schemes in history have varied only slightly – mostly because the old ones are still working. The message of our culture, and the temptation of many in the Bible, is that we should trust ourselves.

Idolatry is the biggest threat to God's children. Idolizing someone or something causes us to ignore God and leave him out of our stories. Not all idolatry looks the same. It might be a golden statue, a foreign king, a shrine to a foreign god, a preconceived notion of what our image should be, or the size of our bank account. Most days in our world it looks like what we see in the mirror. God can work with our weakness and our imperfection. He is not afraid of our doubt. He is not limited by our perspective or our past. But our pride and arrogance, our trust in anything other than him, can separate us from him because it denies the truth about who he is and who we are.

How often have you known that what you were choosing was not pleasing to God, but pursued it anyway? When is the last time you were certain that your plan would work out better than God's plan? When have you felt a nudge to do something that did not fit your agenda? When has God led you in a direction that gave no promise of a happy ending? That just seemed too hard or required effort beyond your capability?

We seek what is easy in the short term; God seeks what is good in the long term. We want to be happy; God wants us to be holy. If God's plan for our lives were based on common sense, Abraham would never have moved out of Ur. Noah would have ignored the whole boat idea. Moses would never have picked up the snake. Peter would never have left a steady job to follow an itinerant preacher. David would have killed Saul when he had the chance, and Esther would have kept her mouth shut about her heritage and let her people be slaughtered. Jacob did steal what not his, but he never owned it. Judas did put his own plan in place, whatever his reasons were, and took his own life when he saw the consequences of that plan.

The stories of the Bible repeatedly show that those who had victory over their enemies trusted God, not themselves.

II Cor 12:9 But he said to me, "My grace is sufficient for you, for my power is made perfect in weakness."

II Chron 20:6 ... "O LORD, God of our fathers, are you not the God who is in heaven? You rule over all the kingdoms of the nations. Power and might are in your hand, and no one can withstand you."

Ps 68:35 You are awesome, O God, in your sanctuary; the God of Israel gives power and strength to his people. Praise be to God!

Rom 4:21 {I am} being fully persuaded that God had power to do what he had promised.

1 Cor 2:5 so that your faith might not rest on men's wisdom, but on God's power.

We may be separated from the people in the Bible by thousands of years and distinct cultural differences, but our sin, our temptations, our fears, and our enemies are no bigger or stronger than those faced by those ordinary people who trusted God enough to obey him. The Bible is full of stories about people just like me....and you. Their stories show that they were tempted by the same excuses we use to leave God out of our stories, to refuse the story he wants to give us, or to settle for more of our ordinary sameness. May we learn from their mistakes and follow their faithful examples to become the extraordinary people God created us to be.

Chapter 1

People like you who don't like what God calls them to do and struggle with pride

There is power in a story. God's Word contains the stories of those who chose to obey him, and the stories of those who chose to trust themselves instead. God's primary command is for us to love him, with all our heart, mind, soul, and strength (Deut 6:5, Deut 10:12, Matt 22:37, Mark 12:30, Luke 10:27). But when we choose to love or obey ourselves or make an idol out of anything, we assume we are smarter than God and are guilty of pride.

Pride is our shortest path away from God. In his book *Serve Strong* author Terry Powell says, "Unless the soul has been tamed, exceptional gifts or impressive accomplishment tend to breed arrogance."[4] Anytime we focus on ourselves, our circumstances, our convenience, or our expectations, we lose sight of who God is and have a distorted perspective of who we are. Pride gives us false security that leads to our destruction, or it convinces us that we are worthless or unacceptable; either way our focus is on ourselves, not on God. Our prideful arrogance convinces us that we will be the exception or that we will succeed because the others who failed were not as wise or clever or strong as we are. Prideful people typically have a high need for control, and they are far more likely to expect to impose change on others than they are to embody that change in themselves. In her book *Jesus Calling* Sarah Young writes "self-sufficiency is a myth perpetuated by pride and temporary success." (April 30) Pride causes us to demand what we do not deserve and to refuse to accept what we do deserve. Charles Stanley writes, "Of all the sins listed in God's word, pride is the most destructive; the truth is that when you are immersed in pride, you rarely consider God at all."[5]

We assume that what we know is all there is to know, that our perspective includes all necessary information, or that our capabilities exceed those of others. We arrogantly convince ourselves that what God says about his people just does not apply to us. When we decide to become our own god, we subjugate the commands and character of God to our own limited, faulty judgment. We give ourselves the last word on what we will or won't do, or how we will modify what God has said to make "obedience" easier or more palatable. Our pride convinces us that we are all we need or that we won't accept what God has promised us…until we find ourselves mired in consequences we would never have chosen, over which we have no control. Our arrogance can cause us to quarrel with God or ignore him altogether, but our arrogance will always separate us from him.

The first four commandments are given to help us remember that he is God, and we are not. God is not surprised by the arrogance of his people, and he wants us to be mindful of that temptation. God intentionally includes the stories of prideful people in his word. We cannot claim ignorance when his Word clearly states the consequences of pride.

Ps 10:4 In his pride the wicked does not seek him; in all his thoughts there is no room for God.

Prov 16:18 Pride goes before destruction, a haughty spirit before a fall.

Prov 29:23 A man's pride brings him low, but a man of lowly spirit gains honor.

Is 2:17 The arrogance of man will be brought low and human pride humbled; the LORD alone will be exalted in that day.

Prov 16:5 The LORD detests all the proud of heart. Be sure of this: They will not go unpunished.

God has defined his people as his bride, his beloved children, and his sheep. He has promised us his presence (Matt 28:20) and his protection (Ps 91:4), and wants to give us abundant life (John 10:10) that will end with "eternal pleasures at his right hand" (Ps 16:11). When we choose to pretend that we are god and he is not, we separate ourselves from his presence and his plans that are intended to bring us good.

Our choice to indulge our pride, whether that looks like an inflated ego or self-deprecation, leads us to sin. We try to justify our sin, but our excuses all come down to whether we focus on God or we focus on ourselves. There are lots of reasons why we choose to trust ourselves more than we trust God. We want to pretend that if God loved us he would never ask us to do something we don't like. Our plan may look easier based on our limited perspective or we may not approve of God's timing or method. We may prefer to avoid situations or people we don't like. We typically prefer the easy way out. We like maximum gain for minimal effort.

God does not do things our way. He is not bound by our rules or our expectations. His goal is not to be our fairy godfather or impress us; his overriding purpose is not to make us happy or make our lives easy and fun; his objective is to help us see him as he is and see ourselves as his beloved children.

We can be angry that God did not obey us and grant our perfectly righteous prayer request, or that he allowed suffering when we asked for relief. We can refuse when he asks us to do something we do not respect or what we consider to be "beneath" us. We can assume we are his favorite and withhold our blessing and mercy from a brother or sister in the family of God, and we can hope that he will not punish us for the same behavior we want him to punish in others. The truth of the matter is that each of us is God's favorite, including the one you do not like.

But the bottom line is that our relationship with God is not negotiable. Delayed obedience and partial obedience are still disobedience, no matter how well we justify and rationalize. When God places a call on our life, we can obey him, or we can obey ourselves.

Most of the chapters in this book are about people in the Bible who provide us examples worthy of emulation. This is not one of those chapters.

Jonah

Sometimes I get frustrated because I want more plot and character analysis than the Bible gives. The book of Jonah is absolutely one of the best examples of a biblical story where I want WAY more detail than is provided. We are given only one "keyhole" glimpse into the heart and life of a man who, frankly, is a pretty poor example of a man of God.

During the eighth century BC when Jonah lived in Israel, there were two main enemies of the Hebrew people: Egypt and Assyria. Maybe Jonah hoped for the acclaim or popularity of a great preacher or the legacy of a great prophet. At the very least he would have wanted to use his calling and his gifts to serve his own people. But he is the only Old Testament prophet called specifically to prophesy outside the nation of Israel. God's call on Jonah's life was to preach to the people of Assyria. Maybe Jonah wanted to preach the sermon that brought about the greatest revival in the Bible…and he did! It's just that he preached it to people that he really hoped would go to hell. God called Jonah to serve the enemy of his people. But Jonah liked his own plan for the destruction of the Ninevites better than he liked God's plan to save them. Before we self-righteously condemn Jonah for his arrogant disobedience to God's specific command, we need to understand what Jonah knew about the Ninevites.

Assyria was ruled intermittently by warring city-states like Sumer, Akkad, and Babylon. During Jonah's lifetime, Nineveh was the capital of Assyria and was located about 200 miles from modern day Baghdad, about a half mile from the Tigris River, near the modern day city of Mosul. The city of Nineveh had public parks, aqueducts, irrigation canals, a palace with eighty rooms and a library with over thirty thousand inscribed tablets.[6]

Despite the sophistication and advances of that culture, archeological evidence indicates that they were also very barbaric. Nineveh was infamous for its cruelty to its enemies. Stone reliefs uncovered by archeologists show men impaled on the city walls with hands and feet piled on the ground and heads stacked on spears. Some court records recount flaying prisoners alive and stacking their skins or burning the bodies of children when their cities were taken. In dealing with prisoners, from their own society and those captured in war, they were known to blind them, cut off limbs, tear out tongues, impale people on poles, burn them alive, bury victims from the neck down in the desert and pull out their tongue and stake it to the ground and leave them to die.[7] Nineveh was easy to hate. They were an idolatrous, evil people who would carry the northern tribes into captivity in 722 BC. The book of Nahum discusses them.

Nah 3:1-3, 19 Woe to the city of blood, full of lies, full of plunder, never without victims! The crack of whips, the clatter of wheels, galloping horses and jolting chariots! Charging cavalry, flashing swords and glittering spears! Many casualties, piles of dead, bodies without number, people stumbling over the corpses— Nothing can heal your wound; your injury is fatal. Everyone who hears the news about you claps his hands at your fall, for who has not felt your endless cruelty?

Isaiah, Amos, and Hosea all prophesied that Assyria would conquer Israel. It is highly probably that Jonah knew these prophecies. Did he hear stories about Nineveh as a child? Had a member of his family member been lost to or tortured by them? Jonah probably not only feared going to the capital city of the empire that threatened his people; he clearly wanted God to destroy them. Jonah's stake in Nineveh wasn't personal yet, but the threat was. Barber sums up Jonah's call. "He was given a ministry he did not want to a people he did not like, and his response was far from spiritual."[8]

The most pious people of his time would have praised Jonah's hatred of these evil people. God didn't agree. God wanted the Jews to understand that, while they are his chosen people, it is their mission to take the gospel of his character and love for his children to all people...even those that they consider to be their enemies.

Jonah 1:1 The word of the LORD came to Jonah son of Amittai: "Go to the great city of Nineveh and preach against it, because its wickedness has come up before me."

It is bad enough that God seemed to ignore the abhorrent evil of the Ninevites, and that God wanted to try to save them, rather than condemn them. But for Jonah, the worst part was that God wanted him to help to save them. However Jonah learned to hate Nineveh, he had to have been aghast when he heard what God wanted him to do. How we respond to what we don't want to hear may be the best indication of what we believe about God. Jonah's response to this incredible command:

Jon 1:3 But Jonah ran away from the LORD and headed for Tarshish. He went down to Joppa, where he found a ship bound for that port. After paying the fare, he went aboard and sailed for Tarshish to flee from the LORD.

Jonah ran from God. He did not want the enemy of his people included in God's love, and he really did not want to be the one to deliver the invitation. He went to the closest port he could find (Joppa – currently a suburb of Tel Aviv), and bought a ticket to the farthest place he could go. Tarshish (off the coast of Spain near Gibraltar) is about 2000 miles in the opposite direction of where God sent him. That ship would have taken at least months, maybe a year to reach Tarshish. This was as far away as he knew how to go.

Lest we smugly disdain Jonah, what would you do if God called you to go be a missionary to a camp of Muslim extremists? How enthusiastic would you be to share your testimony with those who behead their enemies on camera or produce videos of burning their prisoners alive? To speak God's Word to gangs who arm and recruit children and teach them to hate and kill and rape? Suppose God's call on your life was to live among ISIS or a drug cartel or MS13 or the Aryan brotherhood? To those who actively practice witchcraft or Satanism? How passionate are you about the salvation of those who have no regard for human life or God? Who intentionally seek the destruction of any who do not believe like they do? Does their need break your heart? Or are you content to let them die in their sin and suffer the hellish consequences of their choices? Sadly, I think most of us have far more in common with Jonah than we are willing to admit.

Jonah boarded a ship that would have most likely been a Phoenician ship. Phoenicia was the first country to have an organized navy, and they were considered the best ship builders and sailors of that time. They were polytheistic and worshipped gods who represented various parts of nature. Ironically, these pagan sailors seem to be far wiser and kinder than Jonah.

God sent a storm that frightened all aboard. The crew threw cargo overboard, trying to keep the ship afloat. They prayed to their gods, they feared Jonah's god, and they desperately tried to avoid endangering Jonah's life. Jonah, on the other hand, did not pray, went below to find a more comfortable place to sleep, and seemed to have no concern for the welfare of the men who were suffering for his disobedience. These pagan sailors were kinder to him than he was to the Ninevites. Jonah has lost his prayer life, his compassion, and his testimony. And it was about to get worse.

They decided to draw lots to try to determine who was responsible for this storm. Usually this was done by rolling dice or bones in order to receive an answer from the pagan gods. Their interpretation of the answer cast the blame Jonah. (It is interesting that God can use common conventions to speak truth!). Jonah's response was not sorrow for all the danger he put the sailors in; he did not cry out to his God; he did not even appear to show fear; he just told them to throw him into the wind and waves of the storm (see vs 11). In Jon 1:13-14 they desperately try to show mercy to the man who is the cause of this whole mess. There is no evidence of repentance or remorse on Jonah's part. He does not tell the truth until he has no other choice. He apparently preferred to risk the lives of those around him or ultimately to kill himself, rather than save Nineveh.

God was not surprised by Jonah's attempted escape. Long before Jonah fell into the sea, God sent a fish to be in just the right place at just the right time to rescue this angry, disobedient, unloving prophet. How far down did Jonah sink before the fish arrived? Did the sailors see the fish? What did they learn from this encounter with God's prophet? For me, the most amazing detail of that particular part of the story is that it took Jonah three days inside that fish before he finally got around to repentance.

God is where we are and he hears us, regardless of the difficulty of our circumstances or the severity of our disobedience. Jon 2:1-9 is Jonah's prayer from inside the fish. He asks God for mercy and grace for himself; he refuses to show that same mercy and grace to his enemies. He intentionally disobeyed and ran away from God; now he asks that same God to deliver him. What has changed? Why is now the first time he prays? He acknowledges that God is omnipresent and realizes that God has caused all that has happened. Jonah's repentance and hope for deliverance in verse 9 had to be based on blind hope; it was impossible for him to foresee a good ending at this point. Only after Jonah admits his disobedience and acknowledges that he is not in charge does God deliver him. The fish is already swimming for shore where he will vomit Jonah out, and Jonah will begin a do-over.

God is sovereign; you will either do his will or you will be outside of his will. Clearly God has complete control of the storm, the lots, and the fish. He does not lose sight of your disobedience. He never stops seeking relationship with you – even when things have to get ugly in order to get your attention. The most amazing thing is all the effort God expends to save Jonah and encourage him to obey. God got Jonah out of the storm.... and into a fish....out of the fish and back to the original plan he tried to desperately to avoid.

At the beginning of chapter 3, God just starts over. He does not lecture Jonah or rub his face in it. God does not even acknowledge that this is a do-over; he just simply restates the exact command he gave in 1:1. Jonah's assignment has not changed, but his perception of God has. The root word of repent means to turn around. That is literally and figuratively what Jonah did.

Why didn't God just give up on Jonah and call someone who was easier to work with? Don't you think God could have found someone, anyone, who would have been less trouble? God did not need Jonah to preach to the Ninevites. God could have spoken to someone in Nineveh that he could have raised up as a prophet there; God could have done some miraculous sign in that city; God could have sent someone else or spoken in a dream to their king. But he didn't. God could have done it without Jonah, but God wanted Jonah to be a part of his plan for Nineveh. This story is not about the salvation of the enemy of Israel; the book of Jonah is about God's efforts to save one of his own, one who claims to be his prophet. This time, when God says "Go to Nineveh", Jonah has learned his lesson.

When Jonah arrived in Nineveh, his clothes and beard would have clearly marked him as a foreigner. He spent three days walking through this enormous city filled with those he counts as his enemies. He gives what is undeniably the shortest, most pathetic, dispassionate attempt at a sermon ever preached....and the greatest revival in the Bible, maybe in history, is accomplished.

Jon 3:4 Jonah began by going a day's journey into the city, proclaiming "Forty more days and Nineveh will be overthrown."

It was not heartfelt or clever or funny or eloquent, but God used it to convert 120,000 people, and typically they only counted the men – boys under a certain age, women and slaves would not have been included in the count. Because of Jonah, the Ninevites believed God. (Jon 3:5) Notice that they heard Jonah, but believed God.

Jon 4:1-5 But Jonah was greatly displease and became angry. He prayed to the Lord, "O Lord, is this not what I said when I was still at home? That is why I was so quick to flee to Tarshish. I knew that you are a gracious and compassionate God, slow to anger and abounding in love, a God who relents from sending calamity. Now O Lord, take away my life, for it is better for me to die than to live." But the Lord replied, "Have you any right to be angry?" Jonah went out and sat down at a place east of the city. There he made himself a shelter, sat in its shade and waited to see what would happen to the city.

He has done the bare minimum of what God commanded him, and he has crossed west to east and exited the city gates on the east side. I suspect he wants a good vantage point to watch what he hopes will be the violent destruction of this city. Jonah was finished with Nineveh, but God was not finished with Jonah. Jonah was disappointed at their repentance and God's mercy – the same mercy that saved him in the fish. Notice that he uses two adjectives to describe God: gracious and compassionate – he has known God's grace and compassion in his own life. He expects God to be merciful to him and to Israel, but he wants to deny God the option of behaving the same way to anyone he doesn't like. Jonah originally ran because he does not want them to be saved. Now he still does not want them to have the same chance he had.

Jon 4:6-11 Then the Lord God provided a vine and made it grow up over Jonah to give shade for his head to ease his discomfort and Jonah was very happy about the vine. But at dawn the next day God provided a worm, which chewed the vine so that it withered. When the sun rose, God provided a scorching east wind, and the sun blazed on Jonah's head so that he grew faint. He wanted to die, and said, "It would be better for me to die than to live." But God said to Jonah, "Do you have a right to be angry about the vine?" "I do," he said. "I am angry enough to die." But the Lord said, "You have been concerned about this vine, though you did not tend it or make it grow. It sprang up overnight and died overnight. But Nineveh has more than a hundred and twenty thousand people who cannot tell their right hand from their left, and many cattle as well. Should I not be concerned about that great city?"

Even after witnessing all God's miracles and power, Jonah refuses to submit himself to God's authority; he still wants God to obey him. Jonah went through the motions of obedience, but he did not allow God's love to flow through him. There is no evidence that Jonah repented or that the revival in Nineveh had lasting effect. The salvation of the city did not make Jonah happy - a vine did. When the vine died and he lost his shade, he unleashed his anger on God. Jonah has another pity party. This is the only control he has left. He decides he would rather die than be a part of a plan he does not like. He clearly trusts his own opinion more than God's sovereignty.

To Nineveh, God sent a second rate preacher with a bad attitude. To Jonah he sent a wind, a storm, a fish, a vine, a worm, and a scorching wind. The people of Nineveh believed in the God they did not really know. Jonah refused to honor the one who rescued him from drowning and from the fish, the one he was supposed to represent.

Jonah is angry because God does not do what Jonah wants him to do. Do not fool yourself. Anytime you dictate to God or get angry with him because he does not obey you, he is no longer your Lord. Having what you believe is a good idea and demanding your way does not give you control over God. He is God; you are not. God's children are not better than everyone else. Christianity is not some exclusive club where we get more access to God and better blessings and a pass on failure, heartache and suffering. On the contrary, our relationship with God makes us more accountable than everyone else; it does not make us better than they are.

Nineveh repented. There is no biblical evidence that Jonah ever did. Part of the plausibility of this book is the brutal honesty at telling the story of an unwilling, disobedient man of God. The Bible is full of incompetent people who do great things trying to please God. Here is the story of man who does not want to please God, and God still uses him to bring about the largest mass conversion recorded in the Bible. God's will in this world is not limited by the disobedient choices of his children. But our arrogant, disobedient choices, our refusal to honor him as lord of our lives and lord over our enemies will limit our own ability to know his peace and presence and to see his power.

A sociology professor told me that by the time we are in our mid 20's, we have made decisions on what we believe, and we spend the rest of our lives looking for proof that we are right. Even if we spend our lives trying to prove ourselves right, God's power in our world will not be diminished. But God's power in us will be. We may very well end up celebrating a pathetic pity party, all alone, while those we oppose may know fellowship and salvation from the God we profess to serve. Ignoring God and following your preferences and best judgment away from God will never end well.

Norman Blackaby defines it like this: "Repentance is not admitting we are wrong in order to avoid the consequences of our sin or God's discipline in our lives. Repentance is a changed heart… "[9] I cannot say whether or not Jonah's prayer from the fish was truly repentance or just an intense regret of the consequences of his choices and circumstances; I can say that there is no discernible change in his character at the end of his story. Tony Evans summarizes Jonah's hypocrisy. "You cannot expect to be a recipient of God's grace and refuse to be a dispenser of it. If you're not willing to dispense it, you won't receive it."[10]

Sadly, all we know about Jonah is what he didn't like. He didn't like his call or where his disobedience took him; he didn't like the people of Nineveh or God's will. He didn't like the hot sun or mercy directed at anyone other than himself. He was willing to work for God as long as he got to be in charge. When he couldn't successfully command God, he refused to be a part of the story God so wanted to give him.

What if he had stayed in Nineveh, discipling the people, teaching them about God, encouraging them to know the one who so desired their repentance? What if his legacy was to create peace between these repentant citizens of Nineveh and use their repentance as an example for the Israelites to repent as well? We will never know. Whether Jonah's choices were based on pure hatred, prejudice, or simply his own pride, he rejected God's attempts to change his mind. His biblical story ends with him pouting in the hot sun. When he refused to accept the ministry God gave him, he lost the blessing that would have come from obedience.

Rich Young Ruler

He is called the "Rich Young Ruler". His wealth, youth, and power are the only details we know about him. His story is in three of the gospels (Matt 19, Mark 10, and Luke 18), but none give his name. His only contribution to biblical record is that he chose to serve his pride, rather than love and trust his God.

> Mark 10:17-22 As Jesus started on his way, a man ran up to him and fell on his knees before him. "Good teacher," he asked, "what must I do to inherit eternal life?" "Why do you call me good?" Jesus answered. "No one is good--except God alone. You know the commandments: 'Do not murder, do not commit adultery, do not steal, do not give false testimony, do not defraud, honor your father and mother.'" "Teacher," he declared, "all these I have kept since I was a boy." Jesus looked at him and loved him. "One thing you lack," he said. "Go, sell everything you have and give to the poor, and you will have treasure in heaven. Then come, follow me." At this the man's face fell. He went away sad, because he had great wealth.

This Rich Young Ruler did so much right!! He ran to Jesus, fell on his knees before him, recognized that Jesus was good, sought his advice, knew the commandments and had obeyed them since he was a boy. He is off to a really good start! But our relationship with God is not just about what we've done in the past; it is about what we choose to do with our relationship with God in our present.

Why would he have asked Jesus that question? Did he truly wonder, or was he hoping to receive public praise? Did he sense there was something lacking in his life, or was this question born of his pride and need for affirmation? What did he know about Jesus before this encounter? If I have a question where the answer really matters, I am not going to poll everyone I meet and go with the majority answer; I am going to ask someone whose wisdom I trust. Why would he have asked this of Jesus, rather than of the High Priest or a different teacher?

Jesus answers his question with another odd question. "Why do you call me good?" I wonder if Jesus saw his pride or was questioning his sincerity. Jesus clearly saw that the man did not recognize Him as the Christ. After reminding him of the commandments, after the Rich Young Ruler's confident assessment of his obedience, Jesus tries to make him understand the difference between a completed "to do" list and the relationship God wants with us.

Jesus' response to him focused on the "One thing you lack". What was his one thing? The Bible doesn't give us the specific answer. Compassion for the poor? Humility? Generosity? Or was it that he didn't love God near as much as his money? Had his money become his god or was he just that insensitive to the needs of those around him? Jesus asked him to give the money away so that God could be first.

It is interesting that he was sad "because he had *great* wealth" (emphasis mine). Maybe with just a little wealth, it would have been easier to give it away; he could have still let God be God. But because it was *great* wealth, he preferred what money could buy him, rather than depend on the one who might or might not give him what he wanted. He did not like Jesus' answer or Jesus' call on his life. He preferred his own plan, rather than God's, and ignored what Jesus told him. Even though he showed deference to Jesus, he refused to honor him as Lord.

He went away "grieved". About what? His sin? The fact that Jesus didn't see him as the star student? That he didn't receive the affirmation he wanted? Grief doesn't necessarily end in repentance. Grief can get stuck in regret or shame; it might be disappointment or just plain heartbreak. You can get lost in your grief and stay there, never to know repentance. Repentance is the conscious choice to acknowledge that God is God and you are not...and base your future choices on that.

His goal was to secure eternal life, not to know God. He saw no sin in himself and believed that he was saved by the laws he chose to obey. In the Matthew account Jesus' response to his question about how to be saved was, "Obey the commandments." The Rich Young Ruler then asked, "Which ones?" (Matt 19:17-18) It is almost as if he is just trying to check off his "how to stay out of hell" to do list. But I am fascinated that the list of commandments Jesus gives him is only a partial list. The Ten Commandments begin with four that govern our relationship with God and then six that govern our relationship with others. The only ones Jesus lists are the last six.

The Rich Young Ruler has confidence that he has taken care of those last six. What Jesus knows is that he has not dealt with the first four. His behavior is not based on his relationship with God, but he is now trying to base his relationship with God on his behavior. The problem here was not his money or even his behavior; the problem was his pride. God is God; you are not. As long as you confuse those two you are outside of God's will....no matter what you do with your money. Doing the right thing for the wrong reasons, obeying in behavior but not in heart, does not earn you brownie points that obligates God to bless you. An unrepentant heart is an unrepentant heart – no matter what your resume looks like.

This man would allow nothing, not the need of the poor, not even God, to separate him from his wealth. Barbara Brown Taylor identifies him as "...the only person in the book of Mark who walks away from an invitation to follow; he is the only wounded one who declines to be healed. He could not believe that the opposite of rich might not be poor, but free."[11] His question was "What must I do to inherit eternal life?" That was his goal. In Matt 19:18 Jesus had commanded "Keep the commandments"; his response "Which ones?" Jesus' answer was basically, "Separate yourself from the things that separate you from me."

But the most telling part of this passage comes in verse 21. "Jesus looked at him and loved him". Jesus saw his good intentions, his pride, and his greed. Jesus knew what choice he would make. Rather than be irritated that this man would choose to impose his own will rather than obey God, Jesus loved him. Jesus told him what was necessary for him to find relationship with God.

Our choices don't have an impact God's love for us, but they do determine whether or not we allow God's story to become our story. God does not ask us to approve his plan or necessarily like what he asks us to do; he says that we must obey...even when we do not like it, even when we do not understand.

Rom 9:20-21 But who are you, O man, to talk back to God? Shall what is formed say to the one who formed it, 'Why did you make me like this?' Does not the potter have the right to make out of the same lump of clay some pottery for noble purposes and some for common use?

Imposing our will, protecting our pride, or manipulating to make sure we maintain control will undoubtedly cost us a front row seat to see the power of God manifested in our lives and in this world. What blessings, what miracles, what affirmation might Jonah or the Rich Young Ruler have seen and known if they had been willing to trust God more than they trusted themselves? Because they chose not to embrace God's call on their lives, neither Jonah nor the Rich Young Ruler knew fellowship with God; both ended their stories alone.

Angie Smith said it best. "I have every right in the world to ask God to intervene if it is still in accordance with the purpose of His will. But I must kneel low before Him in humble submission, recognizing that at the end of the day, it just might not look the way I want it to."[12] Whether or not it looks the way we like does not change the fact that God does not ask us to bless his plans; he commands that we obey them. Ignoring God will not change his plans or his call on our lives, but it will change us into less than obedience can make us.

Chapter 2

People like you who aren't qualified to do what God calls them to do and struggle with insecurity

If God were dependent on our capabilities to work his will in our world, he'd have just stuck with the angels. They praise him perfectly and always obey. They were already doing his will in heaven. But for reasons known only to God, he chose to create humans. God has always chosen to work his will through ordinary people who are prone to disobedience and sin, whose spiritual weakness and fleshly temptations lead them to be far less than what God created them to be. One of my favorite things about God is that he sees us as we can be when we depend on him, rather than who we are in our own strength.

Over and over in biblical history we see God call incredibly ordinary people to do extraordinary things. The success of his plan is never based on the capabilities of those he calls; it is based on his own power displayed through them. Paul references this idea in Phil 4:13 "I can do all things through Christ who strengthens me."

It is to Satan's advantage that you doubt yourself so much that you cannot trust God. Satan can use that insecurity to keep you, not only from obedience, but from relationship with God and victory in your daily life. In her book *What Happens When Women Say Yes to God* Lisa TerKeurst says, "I am convinced that Satan wants to keep my perspective in a place where my heart is discouraged and my mind is questioning God."[13]

How big and powerful do you think God is? It is easy to acknowledge God's power when it works in and for other people. It becomes much more difficult to trust his power in your own life when you fully understand your limitations. The severity of your circumstances and the power of your enemy can eclipse your trust in anything except your own imperfection and vulnerability. Is God bigger than my enemy? Stronger than my weakness? Wiser than my uncertainty? Can God actually bring good from bad? Can God bring good from me? Can God bring victory where I see no hope?

When we place our confidence in ourselves and our capabilities, we indicate that we don't trust God to be who he says he is, to do for us what he has done for others, or to accomplish His will in the future as he has in the past. The antidote to insecurity is not just being more determined and trying harder so you can have more faith in yourself; it is choosing to believe in God more than you believe in yourself.

Insecurity is rooted in fear. All sorts of fears fuel our insecurity: fear that we will fail or look foolish, fear that we will be disappointed or rejected, fear that we will face persecution or shame. When we assume that God's calling on our lives is dependent on our capabilities, it indicates that we depend on ourselves, not on God. When we allow our choices to be controlled by our insecurity, we make God's plan and power subordinate to our capabilities.

In Beth Moore's book *So Long Insecurity* she describes a crisis she had with God where he forced her to confront her worst fears. "I wanted reassurances, like, 'I will never let any of those things happen to you.' I sensed him continue the interaction despite my bewilderment and my dread." When she felt God push her past her fear into what might happen if her fears became reality,

> I saw myself getting the news I feared most, bawling my eyes out, grieving a loss, or going through all the emotions of betrayal. The tears stung in my eyes. Butterflies flew to my stomach. My insides turned out. But something odd happened…That's when I figured out what God was after. He and I both knew what I would do. I would be devastated at first. I would probably sin in my anger and say all sorts of things and act all sorts of ways I would live

to regret. I would feel inexpressibly lonely and rejected and probably old and ugly. But I knew that finally I'd go facedown before God just as I have a hundred other times, accept his grace and mercy, believe Him to take up my cause and work it together for good, and then I would get up and choose to live…he knew I had pictured the devastation and defeat over and over, but I have never gotten any further than that in my imagination. It was as if He said, 'As long as you're going to borrow trouble on the future, why don't you just go ahead and borrow the grace to go with it and see yourself back up on your feet, defying your enemy's odds…just as you and I have done a dozen other times."[14]

What impact has the phrase "I can't" had on the course of your life? When have you refused to move forward because you felt incapable of the next step? When you had no control over the next step? The biggest, most dramatic moments in the Bible were not attended by those who had graduated seminary and stopped sinning; they were accomplished in the lives of those who chose to trust God more than they trusted themselves.

I googled the phrase "God doesn't call the qualified; he qualifies the called." It seems that it can be specifically tied to no one particular person or author; it is tied to many, many who focused on what God could do with their future, rather than what they had made of their past. Those that move forward in obedience and trust God to equip them for whatever is to come find that their personal qualifications are not necessary for God to work miracles in and through them.

When Satan can trap us in dread of "worst case scenarios", he can keep us from moving forward. Rehearsing in our minds what might go wrong can keep us from accomplishing anything, including obeying God. But rehearsing what God has done in the past can give you enough courage to trust him for one more step. Reminding yourself of your "Ebenezers", the times in your life where God clearly gave you victory you did not earn for yourself, may help you trust him for the new challenge in your path.

God does not need you; he wants you. He is up to something new in your world, and he wants you to be a part of it. If you refuse to follow him into places and circumstances you cannot control, you will miss his glory here on earth. If you assume he is just not powerful enough to equip you to be obedient, someone else will get your front row seat to his story in your lifetime.

Nehemiah

It was common practice for the rulers of Mesopotamia to conquer an area and carry the best and brightest back to their home country. That is just what happened in 586 BC when Babylon utterly defeated what was left of Israel.

Nehemiah was most likely born to a Jewish family in that captivity. He seems to have been a very gifted, good man, but his qualifications had no relevance to what God called him to do. He lived in the royal palace in Susa, the capital city of Persia (modern day Iran), about 150 miles east of the Tigris river. Somehow this Jewish man became the wine taster in the court of King Artaxerxes I. His job was to protect the life of the king who held his people captive. This position indicated a high degree of trust and was commonly used as a precursor to a position of greater power within the royal administration. Nehemiah would have had daily contact with the royal family and would have undoubtedly enjoyed a luxurious lifestyle.

We know nothing of his childhood, but it is clear that someone who raised him instilled in him a love for the city of Jerusalem and the people of God.

Neh 1:1-4 The words of Nehemiah son of Hakaliah: In the month of Kislev in the twentieth year, while I was in the citadel of Susa, Hanani, one of my brothers, came from Judah with some other men, and I questioned them about the Jewish remnant that had survived the exile, and also about Jerusalem. They said to me, "Those who survived the exile and are back in the province are in great trouble and disgrace. The wall of Jerusalem is broken down, and its gates have been burned with fire." When I heard these things, I sat down and wept. For some days I mourned and fasted and prayed before the God of heaven.

Notice that the wall and gates become a focus for him before he ever leaves Persia. The mental picture of the devastation of a place he had probably never seen made him weep, mourn, and fast for days. Was this deep passion a sudden calling of God on this man's heart and life, or was it the culmination of the influence of the devout people in his life? God is capable, not only of equipping his servants to accomplish his will, but of giving them the passion to begin. Nehemiah set a great example by taking this pain and passion to God.

Neh 1:5-11 Then I said: "Lord, the God of heaven, the great and awesome God, who keeps his covenant of love with those who love him and keep his commandments, let your ear be attentive and your eyes open to hear the prayer your servant is praying before you day and night for your servants, the people of Israel. I confess the sins we Israelites, including myself and my father's family, have committed against you. We have acted very wickedly toward you. We have not obeyed the commands, decrees and laws you gave your servant Moses. Remember the instruction you gave your servant Moses, saying, 'If you are unfaithful, I will scatter you among the nations, but if you return to me and obey my commands, then even if your exiled people are at the farthest horizon, I will gather them from there and bring them to the place I have chosen as a dwelling for my Name.' They are your servants and your people, whom you redeemed by your great strength and your mighty hand. Lord, let your ear be attentive to the prayer of this your servant and to the prayer of your servants who delight in revering your name. Give your servant success today by granting him favor in the presence of this man."

I am awed by Nehemiah's passion and honesty about the disobedience of his people. I love the fact that he rehearses God's promises and claims them. But in the last sentence of his prayer, Nehemiah seems to drive off the map. "Make Your servant successful today and grant him compassion before this man." Clearly, his time of weeping and praying and fasting has formulated a plan in his mind. What success is he asking for and whose compassion is required to get it? What has happened in the heart of this wine taster? His prayers have given root to God's plan for his life; now he is asking God to help him accomplish it.

If you read the book of Nehemiah, you will find that the plan is for him to leave the palace in Susa, travel more than 750 miles back to

Jerusalem and rebuild the wall around the city that is in complete ruins. He is not a priest or a prophet who works dramatic miracles; he is just a layman. He is a wine taster, not a construction engineer. He does not have the knowledge, equipment, or permission he needs to accomplish this plan God has laid on his heart. But God does not need Nehemiah's capabilities; God wants Nehemiah to be a part of his plan.

After he has prayed to know God's will and for God to grant him favor before "this man", one day without warning the moment he had been praying for came.

> Neh 2:1b-5 I took the wine and gave it to the king. I had not been sad in his presence before, so the king asked me, "Why does your face look so sad when you are not ill? This is nothing but sadness of heart." I was very much afraid, but I said to the king, "May the king live forever! Why should my face not look sad when the city where my fathers are buried lies in ruins, and its gates have been destroyed by fire?" Then the king said to me, "What is it you want?" Then I prayed to the God of heaven, and I answered the king, "If it pleases the king, and if your servant has found favor in his sight, let him send me to the city in Judah, where my fathers are buried so that I may rebuild it."

I love the fact that once the king asked him the question, he prayed before he answered. How might the lives of those who seek to please God be different if they were more often characterized by prayer before speaking!! In her study of Nehemiah, Kelly Minter says, "God was always his first stop; action always followed; it never led."[15] This is his moment; this is what he's been praying about for months. And the amazing result is that this wine taster, who has the sympathy of the king of Persia, asks for and is given all he will need to return to Judah and build a wall around the ruins of a city he has probably never seen. Nehemiah gets permission to temporarily leave his job in the palace, letters of safe passage through countries that are hostile to Judah, lumber from the king's forest, and the title of Governor of Syria. He returned to Jerusalem with the supplies and political power necessary to accomplish his mission. The Babylonian army destroyed the city; Babylon was conquered by Persia; now Persia is going to help rebuild what Babylon destroyed.

There is a part of me that wishes the rest of Nehemiah's story could be summed up with "and he lived happily ever after", but that's not the case.

Just because Nehemiah has embraced the burden God laid on his heart and been obedient to set the plan in motion, does not mean that there was no struggle to come. He continued to face his own ignorance of building and the opposition of foreign kings and local, Judean leaders. Most were suspicious of him; many actively opposed him and tried to sabotage the wall. Nehemiah had clear understanding of who his enemies were and asked God, not to destroy his enemies, but to strengthen him for the task. (Neh 6:9) And God did.

I am fascinated that God had them begin with the wall, not a new Temple, or a grand entrance gate, not a marketplace or an army fort… the wall. When Nehemiah finally arrived in Jerusalem, the rubble in the streets was so thick in some places that his horse could not get through.

Walls are built to keep some things out and other things in. We build fences in our yards to give our children and pets a safe place to play. We build walls around certain buildings to prevent those who intend harm from getting in. We build homes with strong walls to protect our families from intruders and from storms. We build walls to provide protection and security for what is inside from what is outside. We have borders that separate our country from Mexico and Canada because the rules on the other side of that separation are different from the rules here. There are famous walls: Great Wall of China, the Berlin Wall, the border between Israel and the Palestinian territory, Hadrian's Wall, the wall of Jericho. All of those were built to maintain separation between what was inside and what was outside.

So why would God have them build a wall around rubble? The enemies of the Hebrews had already taken everything of value out of the city. The few people left in the city were free to come and go as they willed. God chose to begin a new story with his people by building a wall that would separate the ruin of their past from all that threatened their new start.

Sanctification is "the process of God's grace by which the believer is separated from sin and becomes dedicated to God's righteousness."[16] God knew that his people needed to be separated from the world so that they could dedicate themselves to him. His holiness cannot coexist with evil; yet he longs to dwell with his people. They had to begin their new start by sanctifying themselves. Their history and this holy city had been defiled by their idolatry and their enemy. God directed them to begin rebuilding the city with a wall that would protect them from outside threats and provide a safe place to begin a new story with his people. They needed to sanctify themselves and their city to God.

There is a difference between a task and a goal. God's task was for them to build a wall, but God's goal was to sanctify them. God did not need a great builder; this was too big a project for one man. What God wanted from Nehemiah was to motivate the people to do it themselves. God gave him the plan and the power to get started, then helped him see that the people themselves would be the best workers. The third chapter of Nehemiah is a list of all the people who helped build the wall. Nehemiah's obedience allowed other "unqualified" people to participate: this wall was built in record time by goldsmiths, perfume makers, sons of local rulers, priests, Levites, temple servants, and merchants. Even girls were included on this construction team.

Nehemiah's obedience led others to participate in God's will to rebuild his city, beginning with the wall. God started with the wall because God knew that wall was the first step toward bringing the people back and rebuilding the Temple where he would again dwell among his people. Nehemiah didn't succeed at rebuilding the wall because he was a well-qualified construction engineer; God equipped Nehemiah with the faith he would need to be obedient while God handled the details of the construction.

Neh 6:15-16 So the wall was completed on the twenty-fifth of Elul, in fifty-two days. When all our enemies heard about this, all the surrounding nations were afraid and lost their self-confidence, because they realized that this work had been done with the help of our God.

Nehemiah's obedience not only gave his enemies a glimpse of his God, but it led others to participate in God's will to rebuild his city, beginning with the wall around the ruins of what used to be the city of Jerusalem. The disobedience and idolatry of the Hebrew people had given Babylon power over them back in 586 BC, but God clearly showed that he had power over those who had ruined the city. The ones who sacked Jerusalem were defeated by the ones who provided all the supplies necessary to rebuild it, and God used the rebuilding process to make himself known to a new generation of his people.

God's call on Nehemiah's life is like his call on ours. He may give us a task, a ministry, or even a trial to provide evidence of his love for us and his power in our lives. But God is far less interested in what we can accomplish for him than he is in having us share the process with him.

Gideon

Jud 6:1-6 Again the Israelites did evil in the eyes of the LORD, and for seven years he gave them into the hands of the Midianites. Because the power of Midian was so oppressive, the Israelites prepared shelters for themselves in mountain clefts, caves and strongholds. Whenever the Israelites planted their crops, the Midianites, Amalekites and other eastern peoples invaded the country. They camped on the land and ruined the crops all the way to Gaza and did not spare a living thing for Israel, neither sheep nor cattle nor donkeys. They came up with their livestock and their tents like swarms of locusts. It was impossible to count the men and their camels; they invaded the land to ravage it. Midian so impoverished the Israelites that they cried out to the LORD for help.

There is a pattern in the book of Judges. The people sin, are oppressed by their enemies, beg God for help, and He raises up a judge to help them find their way back to him. During Gideon's lifetime, the Midianites were the enemy most feared by the Hebrew people. The Midianites were powerful and too numerous to count. They were so powerful an enemy that Israel had stopped fighting them; they just hid when the attackers showed up. Notice that it does not even say the enemy stole all the crops and livestock – sometimes they just destroyed them. They "spared" nothing "all the way to Gaza".

Midianites typically fought on camel back. This allowed their attacks to be much quicker and gave them a height advantage during the battle. Israel was basically powerless before them.[17] After seven years of persecution by the Midianites, Israel called out to God, and God called on Gideon.

Jud 6:11-15 The angel of the LORD came and sat down under the oak in Ophrah that belonged to Joash the Abiezrite, where his son Gideon was threshing wheat in a winepress to keep it from the Midianites.

When the angel of the LORD appeared to Gideon, he said, "The LORD is with you, mighty warrior." "But sir," Gideon replied, "if the LORD is with us, why has all this happened to us? Where are all his wonders that our fathers told us about when they said, 'Did not the LORD bring us up out of Egypt?' But now the LORD has abandoned us and put us into the hand of Midian." The LORD turned to him and said, "Go in the strength you have and save Israel out of Midian's hand. Am I not sending you?" "But Lord," Gideon asked, "how can I save Israel? My clan is the weakest in Manasseh, and I am the least in my family."

God's response to the power of the enemy of his people was to recruit the youngest member of the weakest clan in the smallest tribe. Gideon's high school superlative would have undoubtedly been "least likely to succeed". He was unremarkable in every way.

Notice that the angel of the Lord sat down under a tree where Gideon was threshing wheat in a wine press. Threshing is best done on a hilltop where a breeze can blow to separate the wheat from the chaff. Minimal hope for a breeze down in a wine press suggests to me that Gideon was probably hiding down there, hoping to retain enough seed to plant for the next year's crop. Gideon was in the midst of doing what had to be done just to get by when God interrupted him.

Wonder how long the angel sat and watched before Gideon noticed he was there? The angel's opening greeting has to be one of the most optimistic in all the Bible. "The Lord is with you, mighty warrior." Gideon looks a lot like a scared farmer, but the angel addressed him as who he could become, not as who he was. There is nothing "mighty" or "warrior" about a frightened farmer, hiding from the enemies of his people, threshing wheat in a wine press where there is almost certainly no wind. God consistently chooses to see his children as they can be when they submit to his authority, rather than who they are in the middle of whatever mess they have made.

Gideon's decisions about how to handle his enemy and survive are made in response to the power of his enemy, without regard to the power of his God. The Israelites' response to their enemies is to hide in caves and mountain strongholds, thresh wheat in a winepress, and struggle to barely survive for seven years.

Gideon has not been dreaming of saving his people. There is no evidence that he has even been praying. On the contrary, he questions God's very presence with his people because of the oppression of the Midianites. Gideon is not all that respectful to this Angel of the Lord, and does not see the irony in the fact that his people are worshipping the gods of their enemy. The idolatry of his people is evident because he has to build an altar to God, and God's first task for him was to tear down the Baal altar and the Asherah pole already built on his father's property. Only his father's clever, quick thinking protects Gideon from the wrath of their neighbors who worship Baal and Asherah at that pagan altar. And with that victory under his belt, Gideon now has a bigger problem.

Jud 6:33-38 Now all the Midianites, Amalekites and other eastern peoples joined forces and crossed over the Jordan and camped in the Valley of Jezreel. Then the Spirit of the LORD came upon Gideon, and he blew a trumpet, summoning the Abiezrites to follow him. He sent messengers throughout Manasseh, calling them to arms, and also into Asher, Zebulun and Naphtali, so that they too went up to meet them. Gideon said to God, "If you will save Israel by my hand as you have promised-- look, I will place a wool fleece on the threshing floor. If there is dew only on the fleece and all the ground is dry, then I will know that you will save Israel by my hand, as you said." And that is what happened. Gideon rose early the next day; he squeezed the fleece and wrung out the dew--a bowlful of water.

Just as his newfound acclaim begins to bolster his confidence, the invaders return. This is not just removing a pagan altar from his father's land and appeasing the anger of his neighbors - this is war. His confidence disappears, and his insecurity threatens his obedience. He proposes a test to make sure God is really serious about putting him in charge of saving Israel. And what an odd test it is! What is his connection to fleece and dew? In a show of incredible mercy, God agrees to this sign that will reassure Gideon of his calling. Then, in a moment of both chutzpah and self-doubt, Gideon then asks for the same test...in reverse.

Jud 6:39-40 Then Gideon said to God, "Do not be angry with me. Let me make just one more request. Allow me one more test with the fleece. This time make the fleece dry and the ground covered with dew."

That night God did so. Only the fleece was dry; all the ground was covered with dew.

This one who fears failure, who doubts his capability and his call, asks God for reassurance again to prove that test #1 wasn't an accident of science. In her study of the life of Gideon, Priscilla Shirer says,

> "Gideon was demonstrating a certain amount of wisdom and maturity by his desire to receive assurance before lunging over the precipice into God's purposes. He was cautious and careful, not wholly doubtful and disbelieving. Gideon was not expressing unbelief in God, which would have surely kindled God's anger, but rather an imperfect faith that needed to be strengthened."[18]

God is loving and patiently leads Gideon to understand that he truly has been chosen. Gideon doesn't trust himself, but God is more interested in Gideon's potential than in his limitations. Both tests involved dew which means at least a two day delay in his obedience. God allows this test because it is about Gideon's confidence, not God's capability. God needed him to have confidence in his call, and Gideon needed to know that God's power was not dependent on his capability.

But in response to these two tests, God now tests Gideon. The confidence of the fleece now needs to translate into his confidence in God.

Jud 7:1-8 Early in the morning, Jerub-Baal (that is, Gideon) and all his men camped at the spring of Harod. The camp of Midian was north of them in the valley near the hill of Moreh. The LORD said to Gideon, "You have too many men for me to deliver Midian into their hands. In order that Israel may not boast against me that her own strength has saved her, announce now to the people, 'Anyone who trembles with fear may turn back and leave Mount Gilead." So twenty-two thousand men left, while ten thousand remained. But the LORD said to Gideon, "There are still too many men. Take them down to the water, and I will sift them for you there. If I say, 'This one shall go with you,' he shall go; but if I say, 'This one shall not go with you,' he shall not go." So Gideon took the men down to the water. There the LORD told him, "Separate those who lap the water with their tongues like a dog from those who kneel down to drink." Three hundred men lapped with their hands to their mouths. All the rest got down on their knees to drink. The LORD said to Gideon, "With the three hundred men that lapped I will save you and give the Midianites into your hands. Let all the other men go, each to his own place." So Gideon sent the rest of the Israelites to their tents but kept the three hundred, who took over the provisions and trumpets of the others.

The Midianites and Amalekites have an army of about 135,000 that is far better equipped and trained than Gideon's army of 32,000. And God requires that Gideon down size his army until he is outnumbered 450:1. God made sure that Gideon was certain of his call; now God requires that Gideon trust God's power.

Jud 7:8b-15 Now the camp of Midian lay below him in the valley. During that night the LORD said to Gideon, "Get up, go down against the camp, because I am going to give it into your hands. If you are afraid to attack, go down to the camp with your servant Purah and listen to what they are saying. Afterward, you will be encouraged to attack the camp." So he and Purah his servant went down to the outposts of the camp. The Midianites, the Amalekites and all the other eastern peoples had settled in the valley, thick as locusts. Their camels could no more be counted than the sand on the seashore. Gideon arrived just as a man was telling a friend his dream. "I had a dream," he was saying. "A round loaf of barley bread came tumbling into the Midianite camp. It struck the tent with such force that the tent overturned and collapsed." His friend responded, "This can be nothing other than the sword of Gideon son of Joash, the Israelite. God has given the Midianites and the whole camp into his hands." When Gideon heard the dream and its interpretation, he worshiped God.

Notice that Gideon's response to "if you are afraid" was not "No, God. We're good on this one...you just give me the cue and we'll attack." Gideon did not ask God for reassurance, but God knew that he needed it. God not only reassured him again, but he proposed that Gideon take Purah with him. They passed enemies and camels too numerous to be counted on their way down the hill, and arrived at a tent just in time to hear a conversation that reassured Gideon that God was in charge and would bring victory to his people. Gideon's response to God's mercy was to worship. (I wonder if he worshiped right there in the enemy camp, or if they climbed back uphill to a safer worship venue?)

To Gideon's credit, once he saw God at work, (two fleeces and one overheard conversation later), he focused on God, not himself. And that is the proper response to insecurity. God's calling on Gideon's life, and on your life, is not about you; it is about God.

As Gideon wakes his men to begin the attack, we see his confidence in God's ability to win this battle by what his men do not have.

Jud 7:16-19 Dividing the three hundred men into three companies, he placed trumpets and empty jars in the hands of all of them, with torches inside. "Watch me," he told them. "Follow my lead. When I get to the edge of the camp, do exactly as I do. When I and all who are with me blow our trumpets, then from all around the camp blow yours and shout, 'For the LORD and for Gideon.'" Gideon and the hundred men with him reached the edge of the camp at the beginning of the middle watch, just after they had changed the guard. They blew their trumpets and broke the jars that were in their hands.

This "mighty warrior" led his men into battle armed with torches and clay jars. (Wonder where they found 300 spare clay jars and trumpets?) While they may have carried swords or daggers on their belts, they carried none in their hands. There was no need. God saw to it that the enemy army destroyed itself. (Jud 7:22) God sent them into battle unarmed; he brought them out unscathed. There is no doubt that the victory in this battle was by God's power, not the competence of his people.

Your lack of confidence may be exactly what God needs to display his power. Our confidence in ourselves, justified or not, may eclipse our ability to trust God. God's power is most evident in those who trust him more than they trust themselves.

God's ability to work in our world is not, and never has been, about the capability of his people. Resumes do not matter with God. Batterson says in his book *All In* "In God's kingdom, calling trumps credentials every time!"[19] God is not deterred by the brokenness of your past, nor is he impressed by your accomplishments. He is never frustrated because he can't find the right person for the job; his specialty is equipping those he calls in ways they cannot even imagine. Moses, the stutterer, spoke for the people of God. A formerly demon possessed man became the first missionary. Women, whose testimony was inadmissible in court, became the first eyewitnesses to the resurrected Christ. God doesn't need people that the world views as capable; he chooses to include people who choose to trust him. He does not need your skills or your intelligence. The success of his plan doesn't depend on your cooperation. Jesus says that the first and greatest commandment is to love God with all your heart. That is all that is required for God to work in you and through you. God promises in scripture that those who seek him with all their hearts will find him.

God requires obedience. His command to Gideon back in Jud 6:14 was to "Go in the strength that you have." You may only have the strength of a wet fleece. You may have the assurance of a conversation meant to bolster your confidence or the passion of a dream or burden God has laid on your heart. Batterson advises, "Do the best you can with what you have where you are."[20] Don't pacify your insecurity. Trust God, not yourself. Go do the best that you can in the strength that you have. Recognize that your courage and strength and your ultimate success are not based on your capabilities; they come directly from God.

Is 41:10 So do not fear, for I am with you; do not be dismayed, for I am your God. I will strengthen you and help you; I will uphold you with my righteous right hand.

Chapter 3

People like you who are afraid of what God calls them to do and struggle with fear

Fear is common in the Bible and in our lives because we live in a post Eden world where evil seeks to destroy what God loves...us. The power of that evil is heralded in our newspaper headlines and on the twenty-four hour news shows. People who chose to ignore God or who pretend they are God can become tools Satan uses to bring suffering and devastation. Terrorists brutally murder, rape, and kidnap innocent people. Our media highlights the tension in our society between people of different nationalities, skin color, and income, encouraging us to focus on our differences and hate and fear each other. Our cities are unsafe. Our youth are being bombarded by violence and promiscuity that result in soaring murder rates and sexual promiscuity and teen pregnancy. The poverty rate continues to rise, family values are disappearing, and many are far more focused on finding loopholes in the law than on personal accountability. Our government wantonly spends money that it does not have, and the security of our economic future looks bleak. And that is just this week. I am afraid of what I see happening to my country and our culture.

But our fears can also be more personal. There is a long list of phobias that cover irrational fears of all sorts of things from spiders to heights to crowds. Many fear that their secrets will be exposed. We fear the possibility of failure, condemnation, shame, or death. Our fear may involve losing our financial security or physical independence. It may be separation from someone we love or losing control over our decisions to someone we do not trust. Our fears are nearly always rooted in the threat of some kind of loss.

We like to feel in control, and fear takes over when we feel that control is threatened. The irony is that our perception of our control is a myth. No matter how carefully we plan or how thoroughly we prepare, things can happen that are completely outside our ability to foresee or control.

Satan intentionally uses evil to threaten us, but he can also paralyze us with fear of what may never happen. In her book *Where Will You Go From Here?* Valorie Burton asserts that fear happens when you are "more focused on what may go wrong than on what may go right."[21] David Jeremiah said, "Our greatest fear is the conditional might – the threat of what might happen. Fear trades in the market of possibility. Or even impossibility, for fear is the tyrant of the imagination."[22] Satan can use your fears to keep you from impeding his progress or to keep you away from God. Fear often paralyzes us because we cannot decide if we should move forward, hide, or run away. We fear the people and institutions that can threaten our control, but too often we do not fear God who has all authority and control.

Fear is a universal condition of life since Adam and Eve left the garden. The KJV uses "Be not afraid" 22 times and "Fear not" 63 times. The NIV uses the phrase "Do not be afraid" 65 times.[23] David Jeremiah researched the word "fear" in the Bible and found it was used more than four hundred times, referring to more than two hundred different people.[24] Being afraid of what God calls you to do is not a new condition unique to your situation, but it may indicate that you do not trust God's power over your circumstances or your enemies.

The people that God uses to change history are not those that have no fear; they are the ones who choose to trust God, despite their fear. All the soldiers in the Hebrew army feared Goliath; yet David trusted God enough to accept his challenge. Elijah trusted God enough to challenge the prophets of Baal; yet he feared Jezebel more than he trusted God. David Jeremiah notes that,

> "Biblical heroes were regular people who had to learn the
> same things you and I have to learn: to drive out fear by
> increasing their knowledge of God, to shift their focus
> from their present fear to the eternal God, to replace

what they didn't know about the future with what they did know about him."[25]

Moses

Some fears are murky, far off, "what if" kind of fears that control our choices because we are afraid of what might happen. On the day Moses met God at the burning bush, his fear was much clearer and more immediate.

Ex 3:1-10 Now Moses was tending the flock of Jethro his father-in-law, the priest of Midian, and he led the flock to the far side of the desert and came to Horeb, the mountain of God. There the angel of the LORD appeared to him in flames of fire from within a bush. Moses saw that though the bush was on fire it did not burn up. So Moses thought, "I will go over and see this strange sight--why the bush does not burn up." When the LORD saw that he had gone over to look, God called to him from within the bush, "Moses! Moses!" And Moses said, "Here I am." "Do not come any closer," God said. "Take off your sandals, for the place where you are standing is holy ground." Then he said, "I am the God of your father, the God of Abraham, the God of Isaac and the God of Jacob." At this, Moses hid his face, because he was afraid to look at God. The LORD said, "I have indeed seen the misery of my people in Egypt. I have heard them crying out because of their slave drivers, and I am concerned about their suffering. So I have come down to rescue them from the hand of the Egyptians and to bring them up out of that land into a good and spacious land, a land flowing with milk and honey... And now the cry of the Israelites has reached me, and I have seen the way the Egyptians are oppressing them. So now, go. I am sending you to Pharaoh to bring my people the Israelites out of Egypt."

After forty years of monotony, watching sheep on the back side of a mountain, God initiated this contact with Moses when he was eighty years old. This meeting was set up by God, but it required Moses to turn aside, and God got right to the point. God reminded Moses that He is holy, that He is the God of Moses' people, that He knows the suffering of his people, and that He is able to deliver them back to the land that He gave to Abraham.

This call on Moses' life is an announcement, not a suggestion. "I am sending you." God sends him back to a place that has banished him to demand that the pharaoh release all the slave labor in his workforce. Moses could hardly have had worse qualifications for this job. The Egyptians want him for murder, the Hebrews do not know him and have no reason to respect him, and shepherding is his only job skill...not to mention the fact that surviving that desert crossing is difficult for a young, well equipped man, and it is highly unlikely that the Pharaoh will enthusiastically support a plan that will undoubtedly devastate the Egyptian economy. Moses has lived a fairly isolated life for forty years, and now God wants him to lead a huge group of people. He tries to use his weakness and the sins of his past as his excuse to ignore God in his present. Originally, Moses' desire to protect the Hebrew people in Egypt caused the murder that began this saga. He ran ahead of God's plan before he was sent; he hid in the desert after he failed; and now he is resisting the call to obey.

In addition to the very logical excuses Moses offered, this eighty year old prince turned shepherd may have given up on doing anything particularly significant with his life, but God has been preparing Moses all along for this exact moment. The timing is as significant for Moses as it is for the political events of Egypt – the old Pharaoh is dead, and the Hebrews are finally seeking help from God.

In his wildest dreams Moses cannot see any good coming from this. Moses desperately tries to dissuade God from this ridiculous plan with a very logical litany of excuses. Highlights of his strategy include questions (Who am I? Who are you? What if they don't believe me?), a perfectly logical assumption that someone who stutters would not be a good spokesman, and then, as a last ditch effort, he just begs God to send someone else (Ex 4:13). It would make so much more sense to send someone eloquent who has some vague hope of not ending up in jail or executed!

Over and over in these two chapters God repeats "I will". I will be with you (3:12), I will stretch out my hand and strike the Egyptians (3:19), I will perform wonders among them (3:20), I will make the Egyptians favorably disposed toward you (3:21). All God is asking of Moses is to go and speak. God promises to handle all the rest. But still Moses hesitates.

Ex 4:1-3 "What if they do not believe me or listen to me and say, 'The LORD did not appear to you'?" Then the LORD said to him, "What is that in your hand?" "A staff," he replied. The LORD said, "Throw it on the ground." Moses threw it on the ground and it became a snake, and he ran from it.

This second forty year period of Moses' life would have been characterized by isolation and poverty, at least in comparison to the activity and wealth he had in Pharaoh's palace. Personal possessions would have been common in the palace; they were most likely rare in Midian. Wouldn't you love to know where he got that staff? He may have even used it as he crossed the desert. He may have found it as he watched the sheep. Did he cut it from a tree because he knew he might need it? Did he carve it as he watched the sheep? Is this staff the one Moses has used for years, or is it a new one? Or did God place it on a path, then lead him to it.... like a present he wouldn't really appreciate until he grew up some more?

This staff is a tool that is crucial to his job. I suspect that this staff was worn off smooth from years of Moses' grip and sweat. If Moses said to one of his boys, "Go get my staff", they knew exactly what he was talking about.

Turning aside to the burning bush required little of Moses. Asking for his staff upped the ante. When God asks for it, that is his first step inside Moses' life and possessions. This is personal property that is really important. I suspect that Moses only had one staff, and he would have used it to climb the mountain, steady himself on rocky terrain, fend off any predators to his sheep, or pull wayward sheep back into the safety of the flock. There is absolutely no reason why God needs Moses' staff, but Moses needs to know God's power. Moses threw his staff down as God commanded. And then things get even worse.

Notice that Moses ran from the snake. You do not spend forty years in the desert and not know a poisonous snake when you see one. He would not run from something he was not afraid of. God does not just do a magic trick here; he confronts Moses with his fear.

Ex 4:4a Then the LORD said to him, "Reach out your hand and take it by the tail."

Throwing down the staff required trust; picking the snake up by the tail was nothing less than blind faith. Why would God give such an incredible command? Did Moses share my irrational fear of snakes? Did he avoid picking up snakes at all? Without question he would have been absolutely sure that if he had to pick up a snake, the tail is NOT the end that you grab! You might have a fighting chance to avoid a snake bite if you picked it up by the head, but picking it up by the tail was sure to end badly. This is Moses' defining moment. This fear threatens his obedience. It is this moment that determines whether he will obey God, or go with his best judgment and gut instinct. Either he trusts God, or he doesn't.

Most scholars agree that this was probably some kind of a pit viper. These snakes typically have long fangs that inject venom deep into skin tissue. Results of venomous bites can include not only pain and swelling of surrounding tissue, but changes in heart rate, vision, muscle movement and paralysis. The venom may cause internal bleeding, necrosis to skin around the bite, damage to the respiratory system and kidney, and possibly even death.[26]

I have to wonder how Moses learned to fear this snake. Has he seen someone who has suffered from and survived this kind of bite? Does he know someone who died because of it?

Ex 4:4b **So Moses reached out and took hold of the snake and it turned back into a staff in his hand.**

I would love to see the video of this moment! What is the look on his face? Terror? Determination? Anticipation? How long does it take him to decide to obey? Does he try to creep up on the snake's tail slowly, or does he violently just grab it? He cannot take on Pharaoh or lead the Hebrews back home to their Promised Land without an unshakable trust in the God who will lead him as he leads them. If he trusts personal experience and what he knows to be true about nature, he will disobey God. Refusing to grab the snake by the tail will prove he trusts his own judgment more than he trusts God's power.

We are not told of how Moses came to know about God, and then to know God. We have no idea what he has learned of God in Egypt, from Jethro, or nature. But we do know that it has been enough for him to trust God more than he fears his circumstances, and this trust begins an awesome relationship. Moses leaves the burning bush with a new job, a new understanding of God, and the staff that he gave to God...that God gave back to him. I wonder if Moses kept a closer eye on it when he gripped the staff, or if it gave him confidence. Did he put it on the far side of the tent as he slept, or did he hold it closer to him? Did he fear it, or was it a source of comfort? Did he throw it down every once in a while just to make sure it still worked?

God took the staff Moses used to walk on rocky terrain and defend his sheep to give Moses confidence and to get Pharaoh's attention...in the throne room, and to turn the Nile red. Later it will bring victory on the battlefield and water from a rock. God took what Moses had and what he feared and he challenged Moses to step out of his comfort zone and make a difference. God took it from him, changed it, and gave it back. That staff was both a symbol of what Moses was and what he would become.

That was Moses' crisis of belief, the moment when he decided whether he would pretend to be his own god, or whether he would acknowledge God for who he claims to be. Facing our fears brings us to the same moment. God is God, and we are not. But our choices reflect whether or not we actually believe that is true. Either Moses trusts God to bring good in his life, or he doesn't. If the snake bites him, at best he will be miserable; at worst he may die. If he does not pick up the snake by the tail, he is disobeying God and has more confidence in his own judgment than in God's control over his circumstances. I think God also uses this as symbolism...he took control over the serpent in Eden, and he still has it. There is nothing that we fear that is beyond his control.

Notice that Moses' reaction is not recorded in scripture, but God's response to his obedience is.

Ex 4:5 "This," said the LORD, "is so that they may believe that the LORD, the God of their fathers--the God of Abraham, the God of Isaac and the God of Jacob--has appeared to you."

Because Moses' trust was greater than his fear, God gives him the ability to reproduce this staff/snake/staff trick for others so that they will believe that God is with him. Because Moses has seen God conquer what he fears once, the next time he is afraid, trust will come a little easier.

God does not need Moses to bring the Hebrews home from Egypt. God can just as easily do it with someone else or all by himself. He could have changed Pharaoh's heart or raised up a leader among the Hebrews in Egypt. But he didn't. God wanted Moses to become all that he had created Moses to be. Once this encounter was over and Moses had committed to be obedient, there was never again any evidence of self-doubt. He never looked back. God transformed him from pampered prince to shepherd to judge and lawgiver. Once he successfully trusted God with the fears of his present, God became the source of his courage to face the fears of his future.

Joshua

When we are in an uncomfortable position that is outside our strengths, we are vulnerable. We may be embarrassed; we may fail. We may "lose face". And whenever we feel vulnerable and face some kind of loss, we will likely feel fear. God called Moses to serve him from his weakness; he stuttered, he was 80 years old, he was wanted for murder in the place God wanted him to go, and he was clearly afraid of that snake. But Joshua is different. God calls Joshua out of his strength.

The first time Moses led the people to the edge of the Promised Land, he sent in twelve spies to report back to the people what they saw. All twelve spies attested to the incredible bounty of the land, but ten of the spies were more terrified of the enemies that occupied that land than confident in the power of their God to subdue those enemies. Joshua and Caleb were the two spies who begged the people to trust God, but the Hebrew people feared the reports of their enemies more than they trusted the reports of the fulfillment of God's promise, so the whole group had to wander in the wilderness for forty years. Joshua and Caleb are the only two men who left Egypt that actually entered the Promised Land.

The second time we see Joshua in scripture is in Exodus 17 during the forty years in the wilderness. This story is about the Hebrew victory over the Amalekites. Joshua fought in the valley with his sword, while Moses prayed. (Ex 17:13) Joshua is the military hero of the Hebrews during their time in the wilderness because of his expertise with his broadsword. Most soldiers would have carried daggers into battle, designed for quick thrusts to mortally injure the enemy. But many scholars believe that the use of the word "sword" here indicates that Joshua used a broadsword. Archeologists have found stone reliefs from ancient Egypt and Mesopotamia concurrent with the time of Joshua that show this kind of sword. Broadswords have wide, long blades and are very heavy, designed for slashing and cutting through armor and bone. These swords would have been slightly curved with a double blade (sharpened on both sides) and were so big and heavy that soldiers most likely held it in both hands as they fought. Only the strongest, most skilled warriors could use a broadsword.

It is unusual to see a real military weapon in the hands of the Hebrews in this early part of the Old Testament. An angel with a flaming sword prevented Adam and Eve from returning to Eden, and Isaac prophesied that Esau would live by the sword as Jacob inherited his birth rite and blessing. But Joshua is the first person identified as actually using a sword. After the time of Joshua, we see some of the judges using unconventional weapons: Samson fought with a donkey's jawbone, and David defeated Goliath with a slingshot. But Joshua was the first actual military warrior to be called by God to lead his people.

Joshua is a very gifted man and successful soldier who was trusted by Moses himself. Joshua went up the mountain with Moses. (Ex 24:13) He would go into the Tent of Meeting with Moses when he spoke with God, and remain there after Moses left. (Ex 33:11) Num 27:18 identifies Joshua as "a man in whom is the spirit"; he had a personal relationship with God. He watched Moses lead the people, and God used that time to train Joshua to become the next leader of the Hebrews after Moses' death. Joshua seems to be the perfect, logical choice. For once, God is going with the guy who has the resume to match the task. The Hebrews have to conquer or drive out the Canaanites and Philistines who now occupied the land God gave them, and God calls their best military man to lead them as they do it. God calls Joshua because of his military strength, but God will require Joshua to use his soldier skills differently than Joshua would have chosen for himself.

The book of Joshua opens with the people arriving at the Promised Land after their forty years in the wilderness. Moses is dead, and Joshua takes over. Receiving a big, difficult calling is scary, but how much more intimidating would this have been for Joshua as he assumed leadership from Moses, the one who dominates so much of the Old Testament and who was so very loved by both God and the people.

> Josh 1:1-2, 5-9 After the death of Moses the servant of the LORD, the LORD said to Joshua son of Nun, Moses' aide: "Moses my servant is dead. Now then, you and all these people, get ready to cross the Jordan River into the land I am about to give to them--to the Israelites... No one will be able to stand up against you all the days of your life. As I was with Moses, so I will be with you; I will never leave you nor forsake you. Be strong and courageous, because you will lead these people to inherit the land I swore to their forefathers to give them. Be strong and very courageous. Be careful to obey all the law my servant Moses gave you; do not turn from it to the right or to the left, that you may be successful wherever you go. Do not let this Book of the Law depart from your mouth; meditate on it day and night, so that you may be careful to do everything written in it. Then you will be prosperous and successful. Have I not commanded you? Be strong and courageous. Do not be terrified; do not be discouraged, for the LORD your God will be with you wherever you go."

God promises Joshua his presence, but five times in these seven verses God addresses Joshua's fear. God does not use words lightly; for him to repeat himself so many times in one conversation indicates to me that Joshua's obedience is threatened by fear. With the repeated command to be courageous and not to be terrified or discouraged, God gives the promise of his presence "I will be with you; I will never leave you nor forsake you." God is not sending Joshua into enemy territory alone; he is going with him. For Joshua and for us, God's presence is the safest place we can be, no matter where that is.

The people have been "on the way" to the Promised Land for the last forty years, and once they get there, everything changes. Manna stops, no more quail, and water will have to come from the wells they conquer or dig for themselves. God has brought them back to the Promised Land; now they have to start feeding themselves. But this land that God gave to Abraham, that Jacob and his sons left four hundred years ago to move to Egypt for food is not empty. Other people have moved in, and now it is the job of these returning Hebrews to retake it.

Joshua's military background gave him good reason to fear the first battle. The first city they encounter after crossing the Jordan is Jericho. It is at the north end of the Dead Sea, and was one of the most heavily fortified cities in the world at that time. Archeological excavation gives evidence that the city was built on a mound with a 12-15 foot retaining wall underneath a mud brick wall that was six feet thick and 20- 26 feet high. The top of the wall would have been approximately forty-six feet above the ground.[27] Against this fortification Joshua will lead people who have no battle experience and only minimal, probably crude, weaponry. He must have spent countless days and endless nights trying to formulate a plan that had any hope of success. He even sent in spies, hoping that they would return with some information about a weakness in the enemy lines or fortification that would facilitate a Hebrew victory.

But as it so often happens, our plan is not God's plan. His spies barely make it through the city gate before they duck into a prostitute's house to hide from the authorities. She then sneaks them back out of the city, after securing a promise of protection for herself and her family. When they return to Joshua, they can offer no more military intelligence than they could observe in the dark from the roof of Rahab's house.

Notice that we never actually see inside Joshua's thoughts…we can guess some of what he is thinking by what God says and what Joshua does, but we do not have any account from Joshua himself.

Josh 5:13 Now when Joshua was near Jericho, he looked up and saw a man standing in front of him with a drawn sword in his hand. Joshua went up to him and asked, "Are you for us or for our enemies?"

The Hebrews were camped just across the Jordan from Jericho, but it does not say that Joshua was in the camp; it says he was near Jericho. Was he outside the safety of his camp, trying to scout out Jericho for himself? Was he by himself? Notice that this "man" carried a drawn sword. He was not casually observing Joshua like the angel who sat under the oak tree and watched Gideon. This "man" intentionally approached and confronted Joshua with the very symbol that has given Joshua confidence – a sword. If Joshua was across the Jordan just scouting around, it is highly unlikely that he would have carried his broadsword, so he is "outgunned" for this encounter. Notice also Joshua's courage as he immediately demands to know whether this "man" is friend or foe. Joshua has probably been worrying about how to carry out this battle, how he can possibly lead this rag tag group of former slaves against the fortress of Jericho, and this "man" identifies himself as the "commander of the army of the Lord" and tells Joshua to take off his sandals because he is on holy ground. (Josh 5:14-15) Angels don't make it holy; only the presence of God does. Most scholars believe this is God himself in the form of a man, a pre-incarnate appearance of Jesus.

So often our fear overtakes us because we think we are the ones in charge. The people look to Joshua to lead them into battle, but the "commander of the army of the Lord" is actually in charge. And the Lord dictated the battle strategy to the warrior he has chosen to lead his people.

Josh 6:2-5 Then the LORD said to Joshua, "See, I have delivered Jericho into your hands, along with its king and its fighting men. March around the city once with all the armed men. Do this for six days. Have seven priests carry trumpets of rams' horns in front of the ark. On the seventh day, march around the city seven times, with the priests blowing the trumpets. When you hear them sound a long blast on the trumpets, have all the people give a loud shout; then the wall of the city will collapse and the people will go up, every man straight in."

This mighty warrior who won his acclaim with his sword and his prowess on the battlefield has just been commanded to lead his people into war. God gives him the battle plan, and the military strategy of this first big battle will basically include a week long parade led by the band. No mention here of swords; just walking laps around the enemy. This will go on for six days until an extra long parade on the seventh day followed by the big cheer at the end. Joshua's response is astounding.

Josh 6:6-7 So Joshua son of Nun called the priests and said to them, "Take up the ark of the covenant of the LORD and have seven priests carry trumpets in front of it." And he ordered the people, "Advance! March around the city, with the armed guard going ahead of the ark of the LORD."

I would love to know what went on in Joshua's head between verse 5 and 6. How much time passed? Back in Josh 1:9 God repeatedly commanded him not to be afraid. Was that the end of his fear? Did he make the decision back then to trust God to be with him like he had seen God be with Moses? Or was his fear the still the subject of his prayers every morning? Was his trust in God so great that his obedience was immediate and confident when he heard the battle plan? Or did this command come from a fearful heart that chose obedience even though he did not see much hope of success? How much time passed between when he received his orders from God and when he repeated those orders to his people? God warned him in chapter one not to be afraid...because of this very moment.

The people of Jericho had heard of the Hebrews' military victories in the wilderness and were terrified. (Josh 2:10-11) When they first saw the approaching Hebrews, they must have panicked. Wonder what they thought when the enemy made one lap around their city and went back across the Jordan to their camp? Wonder what they thought after day two? Wonder how many days passed before the people of Jericho began hurling down taunts (and heaven only knows what else!) at these odd people who walked around their city every day? The Hebrews must have become a laughingstock to the people of Jericho, long before the week was over.

Joshua certainly feared being defeated by his enemies in battle, but I suspect enduring the ridicule of his army by his enemy was worse. Did the Hebrews begin to question the leadership of this new guy? Did they complain because he clearly "was no Moses"? He spent an entire week pursuing a plan that gave no indication of power over the enemy, and gave his enemies, both behind the walls of Jericho and within the Hebrew camp, ammunition to slander him. Wouldn't you love to have heard Joshua's prayers during this week? Wouldn't you love to know how God reassured him and encouraged him during this week? How many times did Joshua replay "Be strong and courageous....I am with you" over and over in his head? How big was the gap between Joshua's fear and his faith? And then the moment of truth...

Josh 6:15-16 **On the seventh day, they got up at daybreak and marched around the city seven times in the same manner, except that on that day they circled the city seven times. The seventh time around, when the priests sounded the trumpet blast, Joshua commanded the people, "Shout! For the LORD has given you the city!**

How much courage that must have taken! Repeating orders is one thing, but proclaiming what you cannot see is other thing entirely. Isn't it interesting that God called Joshua, the military leader, not to create battle strategy or even to use his broadsword in battle, but to be obedient to a plan that absolutely contradicts the most basic strategy taught in any military history class.

God was far less interested in logic than he was in manifesting his power to his people and to their enemies. God does not call us to trust him because he needs our expertise or is dependent on our capability; he calls us to trust him because he wants us to have a front row seat to see his power manifested in our world. The God who will not conform to our expectations is not limited by our skill or imagination. He chooses to include us in his plan so that others can see him in us.

What went through Joshua's mind as the cracks began to appear in the walls? Was he relieved? Surprised? Was he impatient to move in and finish the battle God had begun? Did he drop to his knees in awe of the God who was more powerful than his enemies and his worst nightmares?

What went through the minds of the Hebrews as they realized that Joshua's obedience to this bizarre plan gave them victory? How many of them apologized for doubting Joshua or repented for doubting God? That battle not only gave the Hebrews their first victory in the Promised Land; it proved to them that God was with Joshua. Joshua's obedience served as an example to the people and began an entirely new phase of their history.

Josh 6:27 **So the LORD was with Joshua, and his fame spread throughout the land.**

This was not just about reclaiming land or defeating the enemy; this was about the people beginning to see and learning to trust the power of their God. This was about God establishing the man he chose to lead his people. Joshua's obedience in the face of his fear bolstered his faith and allowed the power of God to be manifested to his people. God did not ask Joshua to figure out how to breach the walls; God wanted Joshua and the people to follow him into the city once the walls came down. How Joshua handled his fear determined what God would do with his future.

God does not promise to always rescue us from what we fear, but he does promise to be with us. Sometimes he protects us from what we fear without our even knowing it. Sometimes God protects us in the midst of what we fear: he stilled the raging storm for the disciples and met Shadrach, Meshach and Abednego inside the fiery furnace.

But sometimes God wants us to face our fears. He can use what we fear to make us stronger and teach us and those around us about his power. God didn't prevent Daniel's enemies from throwing him into the lion's den. Daniel had to have been terrified when he was lowered in to the lions' den, but the next morning Daniel's night with the lions showed the king the power of Daniel's God. Daniel's testimony on the back side of his fear changed the heart of his king and resulted in the destruction of those who opposed him.

Dan 6:19-27 At the first light of dawn, the king got up and hurried to the lions' den. When he came near the den, he called to Daniel in an anguished voice, "Daniel, servant of the living God, has your God, whom you serve continually, been able to rescue you from the lions?" Daniel answered, "O king, live forever! My God sent his angel, and he shut the mouths of the lions. They have not hurt me, because I was found innocent in his sight. Nor have I ever done any wrong before you, O king." The king was overjoyed and gave orders to lift Daniel out of the den. And when Daniel was lifted from the den, no wound was found on him, because he had trusted in his God. At the king's command, the men who had falsely accused Daniel were brought in and thrown into the lions' den, along with their wives and children. And before they reached the floor of the den, the lions overpowered them and crushed all their bones. Then King Darius wrote to all the peoples, nations and men of every language throughout the land: "May you prosper greatly! I issue a decree that in every part of my kingdom people must fear and reverence the God of Daniel. For he is the living God and he endures forever; his kingdom will not be destroyed, his dominion will never end. He rescues and he saves; he performs signs and wonders in the heavens and on the earth. He has rescued Daniel from the power of the lions."

Fear is a tool that Satan will try to use to inhibit or destroy you. Your response to your fear, not the fear itself, is what makes the difference. In his book *Future Grace* John Piper says

> "...anxiety is a condition of the heart that gives rise
> to many other sinful states of mind...Anxiety about

finances can give rue to coveting and greed and hoarding and stealing. Anxiety about succeeding at some task can make you irritable and abrupt and surly. Anxiety about relationships can make you withdrawn and indifferent and uncaring about other people. Anxiety about how some will respond to you can make you cover over the truth and lie about things. So if anxiety could be conquered, a mortal blow would be struck to many other sins."[28]

In direct contrast, John MacArthur said, God can even use "the wicked actions of sinful people to accomplish His will."[29] What Satan intends to oppose us, what we see as a stumbling block, may become the very tool God uses to give us victory. So often we are so intimidated by the size and strength of the "walls" we face that we forget that God has already won the battle. We assume that if we can't foresee a "happy ending", God can't think of one either.

I recently saw a video of a bear cub in Alaska that spied a mountain lion across the valley. Knowing he was in danger, the bear cub immediately began to run. Because of the speed of the mountain lion, eventually they were face to face on a branch stretching across a stream. Just as the lion was about to attack, the branch broke and fell into the water. At first I thought the cub was safe, but the mountain lion quickly moved down stream to catch the cub as it floated right to her in the current. The mountain lion reached out and smacked the cub across the face with her claws. As blood began to stream from the cub's face, I considered turning off the video because I cannot stand to watch an animal suffer. But I hesitated just long enough to see the mountain lion's ears go flat against her head. Anyone who knows cats know that signals fear. Suddenly the mountain lion just turns and leaves. The bear cub still stands on the rock, defiantly bleeding. And the camera angle shifts...to show that the cub's giant mother is behind him. He does not know she is there, but her presence saved him. That cub had never been out of her sight or her protection; his enemy had hurt him, but would not be able to destroy him because he belonged to one who was powerful enough to save him.

How many times does our courage fail when we just cannot formulate a happy ending option for our current circumstances? God does not call us to figure it out and give him suggestions. God promises that if we will obey, he will be with us. God's plan for this world certainly does not depend on our capability; God doesn't need us and could probably make things work a lot more simply without us, but in his incredible mercy he chooses to include us, especially when our weakness allows his glory to be evident. It is no shock that the best soldier is called to lead the Hebrew people into battle; it is blind faith that allows him to trust a crazy plan that shows the Hebrews and the people of Jericho the absolute power of the Living God.

In her book *Chase* Jennie Allen reminds us "Courage for the impossible is most often built by God growing our faith in him in the everyday."[30] Ignoring our fears will not make them go away; it will give them more power over us. How we handle our "little" fears, how we respond to the "everyday" threats, gives us the courage we will need to trust God when we come upon our "well-fortified cities".

God never promised a "fear free" life, but he does promise his presence as we face our fears. If we trust God to be who he says he is, if we choose obedience in the face of our fears, we are never alone. We are not dependent on our capability or talent; we face our enemy, whatever he looks like on that particular day, with the power of God.

Hag 2:5 ...my Spirit remains in your midst. Fear not.

Chapter 4

People like you who are disappointed in God and struggle to obey God when God doesn't obey them

What do you do when you want to believe, but what you've been taught is different from what happens? What happens when the Bible stories and the Sunday School answers do not explain or alleviate suffering? When the God who can...doesn't? When God doesn't obey our plans or conform to our timetable? When he doesn't protect us from what we fear or rescue us from what brings us pain? When the doctor's report confirms your worst fears? When the phone rings in the middle of the night and your world is shattered? When you are fired to make room for one less qualified, but more politically correct? How do you respond when injustice leaves the distant headlines and becomes your pink slip, your crisis, your heartbreak? When you pray and pray and still there is no respite, no relief, no rescue, no miracle? How can a good God allow his children to grieve, to languish, to beg for an answer that doesn't come?

Randall Lolley, a pastor and former president of Southeastern Baptist Theological Seminary preached a sermon at my church: "When the Seagull Doesn't Come". He recounted the story of Eddie Rickenbacker who was a pilot in WWI. He and his crew were shot down over the Pacific and spent eight days on a life raft with no protection from the sun, no food, and no fresh water. They prayed for a miracle...and the sea was quiet. No airplanes searching for them, no boats to rescue them. But later, as he dozed, a seagull landed on the side of the raft. He and his crew were able to grab it and kill it, using its meat for food, and the intestines as bait to fish for more food. Dr. Lolley readily acknowledged God's miraculous hand in sustaining these men until they were rescued, but Lolley's cousin had just been killed in the same war. There was no rescue for him. What does it mean when "The seagull doesn't come" for you?

Charles Stanley defines disappointment as "an emotional response to some failed expectation."[31] Insisting that God conform to our expectations sets us up for disappointment. If we're honest, we've all been disappointed in God. We prayed for a healthy child, and we got a special needs child. We prayed over our children, and they have still made self-destructive decisions. We asked God for healing, but he allowed suffering instead. We asked God to save a certain situation or relationship, and he made us let it go. We want God to obey us, but he requires us to obey him when we don't understand the big picture, when we want rescue rather than victory, when he's more interested in establishing our strength than in providing our comfort.

One of the by-products of sin in the Garden of Eden is disappointment. Sin in Eden cost us our ability to consistently see him as God and us as "not God". Whenever we confuse those two, we are going to end up disappointed. Philip Yancey addresses the problem of Christians being disappointed in God. "True atheists do not, I presume, feel disappointed in God. They expect nothing and receive nothing. But those who commit their lives to God, no matter what, instinctively expect something in return. Are those expectations wrong?"[32]

Even when we know that our plans are short sighted and our expectations are immature, we are still disappointed when God doesn't do things our way. We believe our past obedience somehow earns us what we want. We want immediate pleasure and ease, and God wants long-term strength and holiness. We see only part of the story, but God sees the ending. If our relationship with God falls apart when he doesn't obey us, then we don't see him as God; we see him as some cosmic fairy godfather who should be focused on granting our wishes.

When God disappoints you, what do you do? Do you assume that God just doesn't really know what he's doing? Isn't paying attention? Is out to get you? Do you assume that Satan just won this one? Do you decide that any God who won't obey you, who doesn't give you exactly what you asked for is no longer worthy of your worship, your attention, your effort?

When a child demands to be rescued from a situation that frightens him, a wise parent may step back and lets that child learn self-confidence. When a child demands the easy way out, the parent may choose to let them learn the value of hard work instead. When a child demands pleasure, the parent recognizes that the child needs to learn the importance and value of sacrifice. God does not punish us by allowing us to go through the hard things; it is in those hard things that we learn and grow and see him most clearly. If we believe that God is all wise and all-knowing and loves us unconditionally, why do we demand that he spare us the hard parts of life? Why do we assume that we know better than he does?

John

For 400 years God did not speak to his people. There were no prophets or angels delivering messages. He did not raise up a judge or miraculously deliver his people from their enemies. But without warning time changed. The New Testament begins with the fulfillment of Old Testament prophecy when an angel confronts Zechariah in the Holy of Holies with God's announcement about the birth of John and God's call on John's life.

Luke 1:13-17 But the angel said to him: "Do not be afraid, Zechariah; your prayer has been heard. Your wife Elizabeth will bear you a son, and you are to give him the name John. He will be a joy and delight to you, and many will rejoice because of his birth, for he will be great in the sight of the Lord. He is never to take wine or other fermented drink, and he will be filled with the Holy Spirit even from birth. Many of the people of Israel will he bring back to the Lord their God. And he will go on before the Lord, in the spirit and power of Elijah, to turn the hearts of the fathers to their children and the disobedient to the wisdom of the righteous--to make ready a people prepared for the Lord."

Like Isaac, Samson, and Samuel, John was a miracle baby. John 1:7 describes his mother as "barren" and both Elizabeth and Zechariah as "well along in years". God's plan for this baby was for him to prepare the people for the coming of the messiah. His call and role in the kingdom were absolutely clear before he was born. He recognized the divinity of Jesus before either of them were born; he leaped in Elizabeth's womb when Mary arrived. (Luke 1:39-44)

When John became a man, he obeyed that calling to prepare the way for the king. Kings then frequently sent heralds ahead of them as they travelled to announce their coming. John began his ministry to prepare for the coming of Jesus' earthly ministry. John did not become a priest like his father; he was a prophet.

Mark 1:1-7 The beginning of the gospel about Jesus Christ, the Son of God. It is written in Isaiah the prophet: "I will send my messenger ahead of you, who will prepare your way-- a voice of one calling in the desert, 'Prepare the way for the Lord, make straight paths for him'." And so John came, baptizing in the desert region and preaching a baptism of repentance for the forgiveness of sins. The whole Judean countryside and all the people of Jerusalem went out to him. Confessing their sins, they were baptized by him in the Jordan River. John wore clothing made of camel's hair, with a leather belt around his waist, and he ate locusts and wild honey.

John summarized his ministry by quoting from the book of Isaiah. His call was to preach repentance and God's forgiveness of sins to those who previously thought being God's chosen people was enough. "He preached with such conviction and authority that some who heard him thought he might actually be the Messiah himself."[33] The Pharisees dedicated themselves to identifying the sin in others; John dedicated himself to helping people identify the sin in themselves. MacArthur points out the irony of the life of John.

> John was a contrast in every respect from his prolonged isolation to his abrupt public appearance, from his rugged wilderness life to his dramatic preaching and baptizing ministry. He was born to a woman that could not have children. He came from a line of priests, but ministered as a prophet. And he reached Jewish society by removing himself from it.[34]

When I was in Israel, our guide was clearly amused that most of us in the west believe that John ate insects. He pointed out to us that the presence of the insect called a locust was too inconsistent to be a staple of any diet, and there was no way to preserve them for future use. He then showed us a seedpod from a locust tree. In Israel, this pod is known as "St. John's bread". The pods are very sweet, like honey, and these are what John would have eaten.

John also baptized, hence the nickname. The baptism he offered was for the forgiveness of sins, not the ritual cleansing that the people were used to. He asked them to acknowledge their sin before God and symbolically illustrate their commitment to a new relationship with God. John's message was clear; he was preparing the way for one yet to come.

John 1:15-34 John testifies concerning him. He cries out, saying, "This was he of whom I said, 'He who comes after me has surpassed me because he was before me.' From the fullness of his grace we have all received one blessing after another. For the law was given through Moses; grace and truth came through Jesus Christ. No one has ever seen God, but God the One and Only, who is at the Father's side, has made him known." Now this was John's testimony when the Jews of Jerusalem sent priests and Levites to ask him who he was. He did not fail to confess, but confessed freely, "I am not the Christ." They asked him, "Then who are you? Are you Elijah?" He said, "I am not." "Are you the Prophet?" He answered, "No." Finally they said, "Who are you? Give us an answer to take back to those who sent us. What do you say about yourself?" John replied in the words of Isaiah the prophet, "I am the voice of one calling in the desert, 'Make straight the way for the Lord'." Now some Pharisees who had been sent questioned him, "Why then do you baptize if you are not the Christ, nor Elijah, nor the Prophet?" "I baptize with water," John replied, "but among you stands one you do not know. He is the one who comes after me, the thongs of whose sandals I am not worthy to untie."

And then, one day without warning, it happened. The one he was sent to precede appeared.

Mat 3:13-17 Then Jesus came from Galilee to the Jordan to be baptized by John. But John tried to deter him, saying, "I need to be baptized by you, and do you come to me?" Jesus replied, "Let it be so for now;

60

it is proper for us to do this to fulfill all righteousness." Then John consented. As soon as Jesus was baptized, he went up out of the water. At that moment heaven was opened, and he saw the Spirit of God descending like a dove and lighting on him. And a voice from heaven said, "This is my Son, whom I love; with him I am well pleased."

John saw the dove and heard the voice. His obedience had led him directly into the presence of God himself. His ministry had prepared the way for the Christ, the Messiah his people had been praying for. I have to wonder if Jesus and John talked about God as they grew up. Did they wander off together at family reunions or walk together as their families traveled to feast days in Jerusalem? Did they pray for each other? God had given John divine understanding en utero; how did John handle that as he was growing up? Did John ever ask Jesus' advice on his ministry or question when Jesus would actually get involved? Or did they grow up apart from each other? Were they living two entirely separate lives, preparing for the moment when Jesus would suddenly appear at the water's edge?

John 10:40-42 Then Jesus went back across the Jordan to the place where John had been baptizing in the early days. Here he stayed and many people came to him. They said, "Though John never performed a miraculous sign, all that John said about this man was true." And in that place many believed in Jesus.

John's job was to prepare the hearts of the people for the coming messiah. Once Jesus appeared and was baptized as he began his public ministry, John began to be less and less important. He had done the job he was called to do, now it was Jesus' turn to take over.

Part of what John had been called to do was to speak truth so people would recognize their sin and repent. Speaking truth that people do not want to hear can make enemies for you. John did not shrink from or mitigate this truth in honor of political correctness, and he made a very powerful enemy.

Mark 6:17-20 For Herod himself had given orders to have John arrested, and he had him bound and put in prison. He did this because of Herodias, his brother Philip's wife, whom he had married. For John had been saying to Herod, "It is not lawful for you to have your brother's wife." So Herodias nursed a grudge against John and wanted to kill him. But she was not able to, because Herod feared John and protected him, knowing him to be a righteous and holy man. When Herod heard John, he was greatly puzzled; yet he liked to listen to him.

Herod, the Roman governor of Galilee, divorced his wife and married his brother's wife. John minced no words in identifying this as adultery and incest, and Herodias wanted him dead. (Isn't it interesting that we so often chose to kill the messenger, rather than dispute the content of the message?)

Herod put John into prison, but feared public backlash if he executed him. John was jailed for telling the truth, for doing what God had called him to do.

Mark 1:14 After John was put in prison, Jesus went into Galilee, proclaiming the good news of God.

Jesus went on about his ministry, seemingly oblivious to John's plight. John had heard the voice and seen the dove and heard about the miracles. But what Jesus was doing did not match what John expected. His job was to help Jesus in his ministry; he couldn't do that from prison. Not only is he no longer a part of the ministry he's given his life to, he is unjustly imprisoned by an evil king who does not want to hear the truth.

Did John hear that Jesus was assembling disciples? Did he wonder why didn't he get to be one? Was he hoping that Jesus' kingdom would be an earthly kingdom that would overthrow the power of Rome...and Herod? John was arrested and taken out of the game, just as Jesus' ministry was taking off. John has done all the preliminary work, and then been replaced and imprisoned.

Was he disappointed by God's lack of intervention in his life? Was he questioning the power of a God who would not save him and let him continue to serve? Did he resent that God would not overpower an evil king? Was he hurt that Jesus did all kinds of miracles for strangers, but couldn't find a miracle for him?

The Bible doesn't explicitly say what John was thinking, but I think we can infer much from what he did. Notice that he still had disciples.

Matt 11:2-6 When John heard in prison what Christ was doing, he sent his disciples to ask him, "Are you the one who was to come, or should we expect someone else?" Jesus replied, "Go back and report to John what you hear and see: The blind receive sight, the lame walk, those who have leprosy are cured, the deaf hear, the dead are raised, and the good news is preached to the poor. Blessed is the man who does not fall away on account of me."

"Are you the one?" Odd question. He had known who Jesus was at the baptism. Why is he questioning now? I suspect it was because he was disappointed in God. God did not reward him for obedience, or punish Herod for evil. God did not do what he wanted God to do. Nothing John had hoped for was actually happening. His prayers for deliverance were not obeyed.

I think John basically understood this when he said, "He must become greater; I must become less." (John 3:30) But sometimes knowing what is coming does not make accepting it any easier. He wanted a place in Jesus' kingdom on earth; God was preparing his place in heaven.

Notice that "John heard in prison what Christ was doing", and Jesus just told John's disciples to simply tell John what he was doing. This would not have been new or different information. It was simply a reminder to carefully consider what he already knew. John, the one who spoke truth into the life of Herod, was now reminded of the truth about Jesus. Jesus' answer to the disciples of John was not exactly a rousing endorsement of John's obedience. There was no praise for what he had done. There was no encouragement or comfort. Jesus did not fuss at John's question; he was not angry at the implications of John's question; he just told them to take the facts back to John.

We do not have further insight into John's thinking. We do not know what his reaction was to what his disciples told him. But I suspect he would have recognized the Old Testament prophecy in Jesus' words. Jesus told them to tell John "the blind receive sight, the lame walk, those who have leprosy are cured, the deaf hear, the dead are raised, and the good news is preached to the poor." (Matt 11:4-5) John, the son of a priest, a man dedicated to his calling as a prophet of God would have known these words. John quoted Isaiah to the Pharisees; now Jesus reminds him of Isaiah's words.

Is 61:1 The Spirit of the Sovereign LORD is on me, because the LORD has anointed me to preach good news to the poor. He has sent me to bind up the brokenhearted, to proclaim freedom for the captives and release from darkness for the prisoners.

Is 35:4-6 say to those with fearful hearts, "Be strong, do not fear; your God will come, he will come with vengeance; with divine retribution he will come to save you." Then will the eyes of the blind be opened and the ears of the deaf unstopped. Then will the lame leap like a deer, and the mute tongue shout for joy. Water will gush forth in the wilderness and streams in the desert.

When Jesus told the disciples of John to tell him what they see, Jesus was reminding John that God's plan was in progress. What God had said he would do, he was doing. It did not look exactly like what John hoped it would be, but God was still in charge. There was no change in John's circumstances, but Jesus wanted to change John's perspective. John had obeyed, and now his job was done.

Mark 6:21-29 Finally the opportune time came. On his birthday Herod gave a banquet for his high officials and military commanders and the leading men of Galilee. When the daughter of Herodias came in and danced, she pleased Herod and his dinner guests. The king said to the girl, "Ask me for anything you want, and I'll give it to you." And he promised her with an oath, "Whatever you ask I will give you, up to half my kingdom." She went out and said to her mother, "What shall I ask for?" "The head of John the Baptist," she answered. At once the girl hurried in to the king with the request: "I want you to give me right now the head of John the Baptist on a platter." The king was greatly distressed, but because of his oaths and his dinner guests, he did not want to refuse her. So he immediately sent an executioner with orders to bring John's head. The man went, beheaded John in the prison, and brought back his head on a platter. He presented it to the girl, and she gave it to her mother. On hearing of this, John's disciples came and took his body and laid it in a tomb.

He was executed by an evil king as the result of a rash promise. Not all his disciples had abandoned him to follow Jesus. Some were left to visit him in prison, to take his question to Jesus, and to bury his body. Matt 14:12 also tells us that after they buried John, they went to tell Jesus.

John MacArthur says this about John: "From the world's point of view, he achieved nothing of lasting value. Rather, he was hated, despised, and decapitated by his enemies. But in terms of divine approval and privilege, no one had ever been given a more noble calling than John."[35] And when John's job was done, God took him home.

God doesn't promise us happiness or worldly acclaim; he doesn't promise to rescue us from the consequences of our choices; he does unequivocally promise his presence for whatever we face, and he promises glory – his and ours. I am so frustrated that biblical narrative leaves out key parts of stories when I want all the details. John sending a question to Jesus is the last we see of him in scripture. But the answer Jesus sent would have reminded John of God's presence and his promise of glory. I would love to know John's thoughts as he heard that he would not get the miracle he wanted. I would love to hear the narrative of God's presence with him as he faced his execution. I would love to hear the tender details of God gently holding him and leading him home. I would love to see the delight on John's face as he entered heaven and heard "Well done, my good and faithful servant." But those details are private – between John and his God. John's story serves as an example for us, but his private time with his God is just that.

Jesus praised John. Luke 7:28 says," I tell you, among those born of women there is no one greater than John…" John obeyed God until his time on earth was done, even when God had a different plan than John might have wanted. It is painful for an earthly parent to disappoint a child who wants what is not his best. How deep is the Father's love for his child as he holds that child, despite his disappointment, and leads him forward – to the next stage of his life or home to heaven.

In his book *All In* Mark Batterson reminds us of an unpleasant truth. "I think we've conveniently forgotten that we were born in the middle of a battlefield. The cosmic battle between good and evil rages all around us all the time, yet we live like it's peacetime."[36] Satan has declared war on God and all those whom God loves. War, by definition, is about destruction. Our expectations, our plans, our dreams are often casualties of that war.

Martha and Mary

John 11:1-3 Now a man named Lazarus was sick. He was from Bethany, the village of Mary and her sister Martha. This Mary, whose brother Lazarus now lay sick, was the same one who poured perfume on the Lord and wiped his feet with her hair. So the sisters sent word to Jesus, "Lord, the one you love is sick."

The sisters didn't send Jesus a command or even a request. They just sent him a fact. "Lord, the one you love is sick." I'm fascinated that they identify their brother as the "one you love". They knew he would know they meant Lazarus.

We don't know exactly how Jesus' relationship with these siblings began, but it is clear that there was deep understanding and fellowship between Jesus, Mary, Martha and Lazarus. How was Jesus' relationship with Lazarus different from his relationship with others so that they characterized him as "the one you love"? Why had Martha originally invited him into their home? Were Jesus and Lazarus friends before that? How did Jesus meet them? How did they get so close? During one visit Martha felt free to demand that Jesus require Mary to help her in the kitchen. (Luke 10:40) Her sister, Mary, had crashed a dinner party and made a scene when she bathed Jesus' feet with expensive nard, which may even have been her dowry (John 12:13). The Bible gives wonderful anecdotal evidence of the deep affection between them, but there is no biblical evidence of how their relationship actually began.

I am very blessed to have a few, deep friendships that celebrate with me, weep with me, and make my needs their own. These are not people who owe me obedience; they are people who choose to be in relationship with me. They know me so well and care so much that when I identify a problem, they automatically know how to respond. My priorities become theirs, and theirs become mine. That is the key to deep, lasting friendships.

I believe this is the kind of relationship Martha and Mary had with Jesus. They believed that by informing him of Lazarus' illness, he would know what to do. His love for their family would override whatever else he had going on, and he would come and make things right again. The fact that they sent word to Jesus indicated that they understood the severity of the illness and their trust in him to come and heal Lazarus. But Jesus did not respond like they wanted him to.

John 11:4-6 When he heard this, Jesus said, "This sickness will not end in death. No, it is for God's glory so that God's Son may be glorified through it." Jesus loved Martha and her sister and Lazarus. Yet when he heard that Lazarus was sick, he stayed where he was two more days.

Why would Jesus, who clearly loved them, ignore their need and pain? Why wouldn't he affirmatively answer a good prayer to save a good man? What kind of friend ignores the opportunity to help? Jesus has healed countless people, and Mary and Martha know it. They may have even witnessed some of those healings. And they're not even asking for themselves; they're asking on behalf of the "one Jesus loves". But Jesus tarries where he is until Lazarus is dead...too late to "heal" him then!

What do we do when we ask God for something good, something godly, and he says "No"? Mary and Martha are a good example of what our response in that situation should look like.

John 11:20-21 When Martha heard that Jesus was coming, she went out to meet him, but Mary stayed at home. "Lord," Martha said to Jesus, "if you had been here, my brother would not have died. But I know that even now God will give you whatever you ask."

Don't you just love the consistency of Martha's character? She is the sister who takes action, whether that means getting lunch prepared and on the table, or going to confront the one who has disappointed her. She is not a woman of mystery; I suspect those around her seldom wondered what she was thinking. She has undoubtedly been in charge of Lazarus' care. She is more than likely physically exhausted and emotionally devastated. What tone of voice does she use? Does she confront him with her grief or with her anger? Does she hug him tightly, trusting him with her pain, or does she stand at a distance, accusing him from behind a newly erected wall of self-protection? She knows Jesus well enough to be honest with him. She doesn't pretend that she is not hurt. She takes her disappointment to him, states what she knows, and the follows it with what she still believes. She just states the facts and waits for his response.

John 11:23-26 Jesus said to her, "Your brother will rise again." Martha answered, "I know he will rise again in the resurrection at the last day." Jesus said to her, "I am the resurrection and the life. He who believes in me will live, even though he dies; and whoever lives and believes in me will never die. Do you believe this?" "Yes, Lord," she told him, "I believe that you are the Christ, the Son of God, who was to come into the world."

Deep grief and disappointment are not typically the prime teachable moment for theological understanding. She wanted his presence, his comfort, his peace, his hope, but he stayed away. She does not want future promises that will do nothing to alleviate her grief or fear right now. Clearly Jesus has discussed the concept of resurrection with her, but she doesn't want hope for then; she wants relief for now.

I love that fact that Jesus doesn't recoil from her grief or dismiss her because she is disappointed with him. I am awed by the God who is big enough to handle my honest disappointment, who is not disappointed in me when I am disappointed in him. He is big enough and loves me enough to walk me through that disappointment to the other side of understanding.

Martha honestly confronts Jesus with her disappointment, "but Mary stayed at home". Mary, the one who sat at his feet and hung on his every word, has to have been devastated that her pain did not matter enough to him to come and save her brother. The one she trusted did not care enough to show up when they needed him. After Martha returns from confronting Jesus, she confronts Mary.

John 11:28-29 And after she had said this, she went back and called her sister Mary aside. "The Teacher is here," she said, "and is asking for you." When Mary heard this, she got up quickly and went to him.

We may never know why Mary chose to stay at home when she first knew Jesus was coming. Was she angry that Jesus had ignored that "the one you love is sick"? Is her grief over Lazarus' death compounded by the fact that Jesus didn't seem to care? Is she trying to punish him or is she hiding from the one who had intensified her pain? Is she staying put, preparing for him to come to her, begging for an apology? Whatever her reasons, when Martha told Mary Jesus had asked for her, those reasons stopped mattering. Mary "quickly" goes to Jesus.

Martha went looking for Jesus and told him exactly what she was thinking. Mary didn't go to him until he called for her. I find it telling that her words to Jesus are exactly the same words Martha used. "Lord, if you'd been here, my brother would not have died." (John 11, verses 21 and 32) I do not believe in coincidences in the scriptures. I suspect the sisters discussed this many times while Lazarus was sick. Did they fervently watch for Jesus' arrival as they watched life ebb out of their brother? Did they comfort each other with "When Jesus gets here, he will save him"? Was the heartbreak of watching their brother die exacerbated by the absence of the one they thought loved him and them? Has their mourning been even more painful because of the one who didn't seem to care? Did they speak those words to each other before they repeated them to Jesus? "If you had been here, he wouldn't have died."

The only wrong thing to do with disappointment is to forsake honesty for façade, or to alienate yourself from God because he won't obey you. God can handle your weakness; he can even handle your honesty; it is your absence that creates the feeling of isolation. Just because he does not "show up" or miraculously say "yes" when you want him to, does not mean he doesn't love you or that he is not in control; it means that he has a different plan. Mark Batterson notes the difference between our immediate wants and our ultimate needs. "We pray as if God's chief objective is our personal comfort. It's not. God's chief objective is his glory."[37]

Jesus was not indifferent to their pain. He left a place where he was relatively safe to go to the home broken by death and disappointment in him. Bethany was close to his enemies. John 11:16 shows that Thomas encouraged the rest of the disciples to accompany him, even though it might cost them all their lives. It was not an easy trip for Jesus, either. When Jesus saw Mary's weeping he was "deeply moved" and "troubled" (John 11:33). When they took him to Lazarus' tomb, Jesus wept. The grief and disappointment and suffering of his friends brought tears to the eyes of the one who would eventually defeat death...but Gethsemane is still in his future. Lazarus' tomb and the pain of Martha and Mary are in the present. And those things bring God to tears.

John 11:38-39 Jesus, once more deeply moved, came to the tomb. It was a cave with a stone laid across the entrance. "Take away the stone," he said. "But, Lord," said Martha, the sister of the dead man, "by this time there is a bad odor, for he has been there four days."

What an odd demand. Wonder if they thought Jesus just wanted to see his friend's dead body? Martha, ever the practical sister, points out the practical implications of this problem. The one who organizes meal preparation and presentation doesn't want to deal with a bad smell. Jesus, God come to earth, is not limited by physical law or subject to our expectations.

John 11:41-43 So they took away the stone. Then Jesus looked up and said, "Father, I thank you that you have heard me. I knew that you always hear me, but I said this for the benefit of the people standing here, that they may believe that you sent me." When he had said this, Jesus called in a loud voice, "Lazarus, come out!"

Jesus talks to his Father out loud, so that the bystanders can hear. He is about to do something huge that will change his ministry and display his divinity. He has seekers and enemies in the crowd. None will leave this tomb unchanged. Some will believe, and others will begin to plot his demise because he is a threat to their personal power. What was Jesus feeling at that point? Joy at reunion with Lazarus? Relief that Mary and Martha wouldn't be mad anymore? Gratitude that he could wipe away their mourning? Anticipation of his own death and resurrection? Sadness at the stubborn pride of those who would use this to destroy him?

I would love to see the video of what happened next: poor Lazarus, still bound by the burial cloths, waddling out of the tomb, shock/awe/worship/disbelief/joy on the faces of family, acquaintances, disciples, and representatives of the Pharisees who watched. Did anyone faint? Scream? Gasp? Clearly no one moved because Jesus had to cue them for what they needed to do next.

John 11:44b Take off the grave clothes and let him go.

Mary and Martha's disappointment when they believed God let them down is absolutely understandable. So is ours. We live in a fallen world where we daily deal with pain and fear and suffering and heartbreak. We worship the God who has all authority, and we feel disappointment when he does not protect us from things that threaten us and hurt us. We can require that God obey us and refuse to speak to him if he does not, but that doesn't change the fact that he is God. He has the big picture and long term goals that may be far more profound than our immediate comfort. Sometimes he chooses to protect us from what we fear; sometimes he chooses to enable us as we defeat what we fear. Always, he is with us. He is big enough to handle our disappointment; he loves us enough to come to us and walk with us through our pain, and allow our lives and our faltering, inconsistent belief to display his glory.

John 11:45 **Therefore many of the Jews who had come to visit Mary, and had seen what Jesus did, put their faith in him.**

This was so much bigger than Martha and Mary, or even Lazarus. Jesus used this to convert new believers. Jesus gave all three of the siblings a testimony that would encourage those around them to trust God like they did. But that wasn't all. This event was "one too many" for the Pharisees.

John 11:53 **So from that day on they plotted to take his life.**

God's answer to their prayers to heal Lazarus did not just cost Martha and Mary four days of heartbreak over their brother's death and disappointment in Jesus; it didn't just allow Jesus to display his complete power over death; it is the event that would eventually cost Jesus his life. Jesus' death on the cross disappointed those who thought he would save them from the power of Rome, but it enabled him to bring the eternal promise of his own resurrection and ours.

When we are disappointed in God's answer to our prayers or his choice not to obey us, we need to choose whether we trust him to continue to be whom he has always been, or whether we trust ourselves to become our own god. John, Martha, and Mary chose to trust what they believed, rather than what they felt. They sought his presence and were honest with him. When we trust God with our disappointment and choose to

71

believe him and trust him anyway, we give him room to display his glory and power in our world. We don't just settle for temporary relief of pain or the thrill of getting our way; we become a part of his solution that is bigger than we can ask or imagine in that moment.

I went with a group of ladies from my church to a women's retreat in Raleigh, NC. We were attending a leadership conference that I hoped would give us new ideas and enthusiasm for the women's ministry of our church. There were so many good classes and speakers, and I wanted our group to have the opportunity to benefit from the entire conference. Before we left, we prayed for God's protection as we traveled. We asked for safety, but what we really wanted was a smooth, uneventful trip that would get us to our conference on time with no problems.

Problems began after lunch. When we got back into our van, it wouldn't start. Repeated attempts yielded no progress. While I called AAA, one of our ladies saw men from the North Carolina Highway Department park near us and asked for their help. One man listened as I tried to start the van, and he said, "Have you kicked the gas tank?" I thought he had lost his mind, but I was desperate because our time was short and my goal was to safely arrive at the conference on time. He lay down in the parking lot and kicked the gas tank while I tried to start the van. No one was surprised when the van continued to not start. Finally, the man from the AAA towing service arrived. He listened to the sound of the engine as I tried to start the van. His response? "Have you kicked the gas tank?" I was fascinated that this seemed to be the *modus operandi* for van repair in North Carolina. I got in the driver's seat, and he lay down in the parking lot where he banged on the gas tank with a lead pipe. To my utter shock, the van started. He told us that the fix might just be temporary. We might make it all the way into Raleigh, or we might only make it a few miles. I reminded God of our prayer in the church parking lot back in Richmond, and we took off once again, certain that God could get us the last thirty miles into Raleigh.

However, about three miles down the road I could tell that the van was losing power...fast. There was an exit ahead, and I told the ladies we were going to have to get off. We coasted down the exit, got into a left turn lane at a busy intersection...and the van completely died. I could not believe that God couldn't handle a fuel tank. I had not asked for a big miracle! I was irritated that we were trying to hear from him and learn how to better serve his church, and he couldn't even get us to the conference on time. I was concerned because these ladies were my responsibility, and my head started spinning, trying to create options for us. How would we get the van fixed? How would we get to the hotel with so many women and all their suitcases? Keeping the van running until we could get to the place we felt God leading us to did not seem like a really big request… certainly minor compared to a lot of miracles. I was clear in my prayer request, and God had not obeyed me.

As we were sitting at the stoplight, blocking traffic, frustrated that we would surely be late, calling AAA for the second time that afternoon, I looked one block farther down the road and saw concrete evidence of God's divine control. Less than two blocks from where we broke down was a GM dealership and an Enterprise Car rental. Two ladies from our group went to rent us another van, while the tow truck took the rest of us to the dealership. I gave the pertinent information to the service department at the dealer to have our fuel pump replaced. They promised we could pick up our van the next day so we would only have to pay one day for rental on the new van.

We could have broken down on the interstate in the middle of nowhere with far too many women and suitcases to fit in the front seat of a tow truck. We could have been stranded on a Saturday when that particular dealership was closed. We could even have gotten to a mechanic that could have repaired the van….with no proximity to a car rental place. But that is not what happened. God got us to the exact spot where we would not only have access to everything we needed, but we could see his hand at work. He was watching, we were protected, and he had bigger plans than we did. I wanted an uneventful trip and a timely arrival at the conference; God wanted us to see his power, his presence, his protection. Many women attended that conference and went home with renewed enthusiasm for ministry in their church. We went home, acutely aware that God has complete control, even when he doesn't obey us. I would have been relieved by an uneventful, timely trip; I was thrilled by a glimpse of the power (and humor!) of God.

People who trust in themselves end up disappointed. I have learned the hard way (and over and over) that I am not smart enough or strong enough to take God's place. I'm not omniscient; I don't know the future; I am not enough. God is who he is, not who we try to make him into, not who we demand that he become. If my relationship with God is based on his obedience to me, then I've put myself in his place and demand that he serves me. Barbara BrownTaylor says, "Our idols are exposed when God refuses to meet our expectations."[38] Obedience is not about insisting that God conform to my expectations; it is about choosing to honor him as God whether or not things work out like I want.

There is no formula that we can follow, no regimen that will guarantee us what we want or think we deserve. God's plan is different for and in each of us. Sheila Walsh said, "God in his sovereign grace, heals some while others remain sick. He raises some from the dead while others die. He releases some from prison while others languish for years – or get executed there."[39] Ultimately we need to understand that he is God and we are not. Just because he doesn't conform to our plan doesn't mean he does not love us or that he is not paying attention or he does not care; it means he has a different plan.

The Bible is full of moments when those who loved God were disappointed in God's plan. So many trusted God for justice and were treated unfairly. Joseph was imprisoned on false charges. John was exiled for preaching the gospel. Paul spent his entire ministry with the "thorn" God could have removed, but didn't. They did what they were supposed to do, but God did not spare them suffering. Each of them chose to be obedient, despite their disappointment, and God's power and glory was manifested through them. How many watched the beating and crucifixion of the one they had hoped would free them from Rome? Jesus could have called down legions to prevent the crucifixion or empowered Peter and his sword to take out the legion sent by Rome, but he didn't. Their hope for a savior seemed to be powerless against the Pharisees' schemes and Roman brutality. They undoubtedly walked away from Calvary, disappointed in the one they trusted.

But, in each case, God had a different plan. The celebration and hope of Easter would not have been possible without the crucifixion. John's Revelation of heaven occurred during his exile. Joseph rose to second in command of Egypt where he could rescue his people because had been imprisoned with the one who gave him access to Pharaoh. Paul's thorn forced him to be dependent on God. What if their response to their disappointment in the temporary had cost them their vision of the eternal? When God doesn't obey us, when he allows adversity or hardship or pain that we want to avoid, we can allow that disappointment to separate us from him, or draw us closer to him. What God teaches during the times we are disappointed can be the moments that give us deeper faith, stronger trust, and a glimpse into the glory of God himself.

What will you do if your "seagull doesn't come"? Will you reject the God who refused to obey your plan, or will you seek his wisdom and his presence for whatever is to come next? What do you do with your disappointment? Will you wallow in self-pity? Will you withdraw from God and try to take over his job? Use it as valid excuse for ignoring him? Or will you take your disappointment to him? Can you place your honest disappointment and pain in his hands and trust him to bring his glory and your good?

If we choose to believe that God is who he says he is, regardless of our circumstances, our disappointment is always temporary, either in this life or eternity. John the Baptist, Mary and Martha took their questions and their disappointment to Jesus. John was executed; Lazarus was brought back from the dead. John's task on earth was done, and he entered the glory of heaven. Mary and Martha saw God's power and glory in a cemetery.

God is big enough to handle your anger and your disappointment, but he is not so small that he must do your bidding when it is outside his will.

Is 55:8 "For my thoughts are not your thoughts, neither are your ways my ways," declares the Lord. "As the heavens are higher than the earth, so are my ways higher than your ways, and my thoughts than your thoughts."

Every once in a while I find myself at the end of my rope. I'm tired of fighting, tired of hoping, tired of trying, tired of continuing to pray for the same things over and over. I've asked God for what I believe is a good, godly thing, and I'm disappointed in his response. If my goal is to get my way, I will be disappointed. How much more disappointing it would be to come to the end of my life, accomplishing nothing of significance, having only an uneventful story to tell, a story that gave me all of my short-sighted expectations and never allowed me to see God's glory. Let me never settle for less than God's ways and thoughts.

The opposite of disappointment is not contentment; it is delight. When there is a gap between what you know and what you are capable of seeing, assume that he will continue to be all that he has always been. Trust him with your honest disappointment. And then give him the chance to walk with you through that disappointment and eventually delight you with his plans that are more than you can ask or imagine.

Ps 37:4 **Delight yourself in the Lord and he will give you the desires of your heart.**

May you always choose to be honest with the one who can handle your disappointment in your current circumstances; may you know the comfort of the one who sacrificed everything to save you, and may you find your way through your disappointment to deeper trust in the one with the power to conquer your enemies and your fears.

Chapter 5

People like you who were betrayed by people they loved and are ruled by their unforgiveness

Betrayal usually comes as a shock. Your security in a relationship fails when your expectations collide with the reality of their hurtful behavior. Your trust was returned with deceit or treachery. They "threw you under the bus" to advance their own agenda. Those who should have loved you back or protected you, violated you and walked away. What you shared in confidence was shared as gossip. You wanted their love, friendship, or respect, and they used you for their own gain. You risked your emotional security, and they intentionally misled you about their intentions. It can be as simple as taking credit for someone else's work, or as complicated as the destruction of a marriage.

Ideally, we will learn from our mistaken judgments and become more tenderhearted and compassionate. But more often we respond to betrayal by choosing not to trust, not to take risks. Our goal shifts from seeking relationship to self-protection. We may build walls to keep others out, or we may try to impose control on others to prevent betrayal from ever happening again. Regardless of our response, we feel pain. It is one thing to be betrayed by an enemy; it is something eminently more painful to be betrayed by someone you love, someone you trusted with your truest self and most vulnerable moments.

Those who have been scarred by betrayal in the past often allow self-protection to control their current relationships. They allow the pain of betrayal to alter their perspective of their current situations and future expectations. When we hold on to the resentment and bitterness of being treated unfairly and allow our pain to fester, it allows our betrayer to continue to rob us of joy and hope and peace, long after the offense is done. Only forgiveness will free us from being controlled by the injustice of our past. Forgiveness is not about the depth of the pain or the circumstances of the affront; it is not based on the worth of the betrayer or even whether or not the betrayer is sorry. Forgiveness is the choice to no longer allow that betrayer to control our attitude or expectations. Forgiveness means we choose to put their offense in God's hands so that ours are now empty, able to receive and respond to what is in our future. We may have to continue to live with the consequences of the betrayal, but we refuse to continue to serve our betrayer.

God is a healer, not a magician. He doesn't zap injustice or unfairness and turn it into righteousness. He redeems us by bringing strength and growth from what is weak and wounded and scarred. It is to his glory that those who love him choose to trust him with injustice. Only he knows what justice looks like and how toxic revenge is in the mind of the one who has been wronged.

Rom 12:19 Do not take revenge, my friends, but leave room for God's wrath, for it is written: "It is mine to avenge; I will repay," says the Lord.
Prov 20:22 Do not say, "I'll pay you back for this wrong!" Wait for the LORD, and he will deliver you.

When we choose to forgive the one who betrayed us, we refuse to define our future with their offense. When we leave their future to God, he can do more than we can ask or imagine in our lives and in the lives of those we chose to forgive.

Joseph

He was his daddy's favorite. He was the eleventh of the twelve sons born to Jacob. His mother, Rachel, Jacob's favorite wife, died giving birth to his little brother, Benjamin. The kindest reading of his story shows that Jacob made no effort to hide his favoritism. He gave a coat of many colors to Joseph – no mention of any gifts to the others. Joseph had dreams that his brothers would one day bow down to him, and he arrogantly shared that prediction with them. He may have been the obnoxious, spoiled little brother; he may have just been clueless and self-absorbed. Either way, the older brothers must have been wounded that Jacob did not love them like he loved this little brother. Their mothers may have pitted them against each other, or Jacob may have had good reason to distance himself from those other brothers. Those details are not in the story, and they must have been painful. However, those details did not free Joseph (and do not free us) to assume that even good, justifiable reasons will excuse malice, bitterness, or revenge.

Clearly, there is jealousy and dysfunction in that family. When Jacob sent Joseph to the fields to check on the brothers, they saw their chance. Gen 37:18 says that when they saw him coming in the distance, they began to plot to kill him, but Reuben convinced them to put him into a dry cistern instead. Did Joseph cry out to them from the pit? Beg? Apologize? Appeal to their compassion for their father? Was he stunned into silence? Abusive? Threatening? Gen 42:21 indicates that years later they still remembered Joseph pleading with them for his life. Did his face or his cries echo in their hearts and minds during the years that followed? Did watching the grief of their father increase their guilt?

When a Midianite caravan passed near them, the brothers sold him as a slave for twenty pieces of silver. (Wonder what they did with the money?) At seventeen years of age, Joseph's life began to go through a series of good news/bad news cycles where he consistently did the right thing and was punished for it. The good news is he obeyed his father's request to check on the safety of his brothers; the bad news is they sold him into slavery. He was taken to Egypt and sold to Potiphar who was the captain of Pharaoh's bodyguard. This was good news because he could have been sold to someone who needed him for hard labor or who was cruel to him. Despite his status as a slave, he demonstrated a good attitude and strong work ethic that allowed him to be promoted to the head of Potiphar's household, answering only to Potiphar himself. The bad news is "Mrs. Potiphar" tried to seduce him. Joseph rejected her advances, but she lied and accused him of trying to rape her. The good news is he did the right thing; the bad news is he went to prison anyway. The good news is he continued to choose to be positive and eventually rose to a leadership position in prison, respected by both guards and other inmates. His position there gave him access to a servant of Pharaoh that could speak on his behalf when the servant was released. The bad news is that servant forgot about him when he was released. The good news is he eventually remembered Joseph when Pharaoh needed a dream interpreted. That dream foretold a famine, and Pharaoh decided Joseph would be the perfect one to prepare the nation of Egypt for that coming famine. He made Joseph second in command of all of Egypt. The resulting famine would eventually bring his brothers to him to ask for food. The good news for Joseph's family was that Jacob knew where to send the ten older brothers to find food. The bad news was that the food they needed was now held by the brother they betrayed. Those brothers had not seen him in approximately thirteen years. Joseph has grown into a man and most likely adopted the Egyptian clothing, beard, and haircut, and they did not recognize him....but he knew them.

Gen 42:3-8 Then ten brothers of Joseph went down to buy grain from Egypt. But Jacob did not send Benjamin, Joseph's brother with the others, because he was afraid that harm might come to him. So Israel's sons were among those who went to buy grain, for the famine was in the land of Canaan also. Now Joseph was the governor of the land, the one who sold grain to all its people. So when Joseph's brothers arrived, they bowed down to him with their faces to the ground. As soon as Joseph saw his brothers, he recognized them but he pretended to be a stranger and spoke harshly to them. "Where do you come from?" he asked. "From the land of Canaan," they replied, "to buy food." Although Joseph recognized his brothers, they did not recognize him.

Joseph had no idea what had happened at home since he was sold into slavery or whether his brothers still despise him. Scripture does not give us specific insight as to what Joseph was thinking and feeling at this point, other than that he intentionally concealed his identity from them. He pretended to use an interpreter to communicate with them so they had no idea he understood what they were saying. My guess is that Joseph wanted to see if they had changed, and he tested them before he trusted them. Because they did not know he could speak their language, he was able to overhear their confession. Joseph was given a glimpse into the grief of his father and the regret of his brothers.

Joseph has been betrayed by his brothers and Potiphar's wife, and has been forgotten by the cupbearer to Pharaoh that promised to help him. At any point in this story, most of us would have fully understood his becoming bitter, blaming God, or being angry with God. Self-pity, withdrawal, resentment, or desire for revenge would seem to me to be perfectly understandable and easily justifiable. But Joseph consistently chose to be defined by what he knew was right, rather than allowing their betrayal and unfair treatment to define his character.

Those who betray can be as trapped in the past as those who are betrayed. In Gen 42 when the brothers confronted Joseph, he accused them of being spies, but they replied that they were "sons of one man". (Gen 42:11) They defined themselves with the relationship that was, and always had been, painful to them. Joseph continued to pretend to question their motives, but they replied that they "were twelve brothers, the sons of one man, who lives in the land of Canaan. The youngest is now with our father, and one is no more." (Gen 42:13) Their response to being accused of spying was to describe their family by the brothers who were not present. Their guilt is obvious. Reuben believed that this accusation may be their punishment for what they did to Joseph. At least thirteen years after they last saw him, they still refer to him in describing their family, and they still expect God to punish them for what they did.

Gen 42:21-25 They said to one another, "Surely we are being punished because of our brother. We saw how distressed he was when he pleaded with us for his life, but you would not listen; that's why this distress has come upon us." Reuben replied, "Didn't I tell you not to sin against the boy? But you wouldn't listen! Now we must give an accounting for his blood." They did not realize that Joseph could understand them, since he was using an interpreter. He turned away from them and began to weep, but then turned back and spoke to them again. He had Simeon taken from them and bound before their eyes. Joseph gave orders to fill their bags with grain, to put each man's silver back in his sack, and to give them provisions for their journey.

Joseph gave them the food they needed and returned the money they brought to pay for the food by hiding it in their sacks. But the best insight we have into his heart involves more than just giving them the food and returning their money; he "turned away from them and wept". I cannot imagine the intense emotion behind those tears. How he must have missed family in a land where he did not belong. He may have had power in Egypt, but Palestine was still his home. How many times had he chosen to put on brave front while he questioned God's plan and his brother's hatred? This encounter brought all the pain of the last thirteen years to the surface. Part of his weeping was acknowledging that pain; part was most likely relief at being reunited with brothers who no longer hated him, and part had to have been awe at God's incredible ability to bring this story full circle. He chose to honor God with his obedience when he did not understand the plan, and then he realized that God had been faithful to him, watching and working all things out for good from the beginning.

When you consider those that have betrayed you and brought you pain or treated you unfairly, what do you wish for them? Joseph had the power to punish them and give them exactly what they deserved. He could have unleashed years of anger and pain and shame and destroyed them. He could have had them enslaved or beaten. But he didn't. He kept Simeon as a guarantee that they would return and bring Benjamin. When they return home, Reuben gives account of what happened in Egypt to his father.

Gen 42:33-38 "Then the man who is lord over the land said to us, 'This is how I will know whether you are honest men: Leave one of your brothers here with me, and take food for your starving households and go. But bring your youngest brother to me so I will know that you are not spies but honest men. Then I will give your brother back to you, and you can trade in the land'." As they were emptying their sacks, there in each man's sack was his pouch of silver! When they and their father saw the money pouches, they were frightened. Their father Jacob said to them, "You have deprived me of my children. Joseph is no more and Simeon is no more, and now you want to take Benjamin. Everything is against me!" Then Reuben said to his father, "You may put both of my sons to death if I do not bring him back to you. Entrust him to my care, and I will bring him back." But Jacob said, "My son will not go down there with you; his brother is dead and he is the only one left. If harm comes to him on the journey you are taking, you will bring my gray head down to the grave in sorrow."

Hear Jacob's pain as he refuses to send Benjamin with them for fear of losing another son. Does Jacob not trust them with Benjamin's safety? Has he ever wondered if the brothers had something to do with Joseph's "death"? Jacob says that Benjamin cannot go because he is the only son he has left…the nine men listening are also his sons, yet they don't seem to count. Jacob is content to let Simeon remain in prison in order to keep Benjamin safe at home. Benjamin's safety matters more to the father than Simeon's freedom. Betrayal runs deep in this family.

Eventually they ran out of food again, and Jacob was forced to allow Benjamin to go with them so that his family would not starve. When they first returned from Egypt, Reuben offered the life of his own sons as guarantee to protect Benjamin; now, as they prepare to go to Egypt again, Judah offers his own life to protect Benjamin. The brothers who originally sold their "competition" into slavery, have now become brothers who offer their own children and lives to protect the one their father loves more.

They packed extra gifts for the man who held their brother Simeon, double the amount of silver to pay for what they brought home last time and what they hope to bring home this time, and "hurry" (Gen 43:15) back to Egypt. When they arrived in Egypt, they made themselves known to Joseph's steward who reunited them with Simeon. The steward then took them to Joseph's house, where they bowed down to him when he arrived. (Gen 44:28) When Joseph recognized Benjamin, he left the room to weep alone.

Eventually, after being completely sure that his older brothers meant neither him nor Benjamin any harm, Joseph was ready to be family again.

Gen 45:1-11 Then Joseph could not control himself before all those who stood by him, and he cried, "Have everyone leave my presence!" So there was no one with Joseph when he made himself known to his brothers. And he wept so loudly that the Egyptians heard it, and the Pharaoh's household heard about it. Joseph said to his brothers, "I am Joseph! Is my father living?" But his brothers were not able to answer him, because they were terrified at his presence. Then Joseph said to his brothers, "Come close to me." When they had done so, he said, "I am your brother Joseph, the one you sold into Egypt. And now do not be distressed and do not be angry with yourselves for selling me here, because it was to save lives that **God sent me** ahead of you. For two years now there has been famine in the land, and for the next five years there will not be plowing and reaping. But **God sent me** ahead of you to preserve for you a remnant on earth and to save your lives by a great deliverance. So then, **it was not you who sent me here, but God**. He made me father to Pharaoh, lord of his entire household and ruler of all Egypt. Now hurry back to my father and say to him, 'this is what your son Joseph says: God has made me lord of all Egypt. Come down to me; don't delay. You shall live in the region of Goshen and be near me – you, your children and grandchildren, your flocks and herds, and all you have. I will provide for you there, because five years of famine are still to come. Otherwise you and your household and all who belong to you will become destitute." (emphasis mine)

Joseph saw God in the midst of his story because he never tried to rewrite his story into something God didn't ordain. Joseph was unjustly treated, undeservedly abused, but he chose to love and forgive; he chose to see his brothers through the eyes of God, rather than through the pain of his betrayal. He recognized that his suffering, at their hand, had led him to the exact place God could use and bless him, from which he could relieve, not only his family's hunger, but their guilt.

I love the fact that he tells them to tell his dad that he has "splendor in Egypt". (Gen 45:13) Boys never outgrow wanting to make their dad proud. He also knows that they will be safest living in Egypt under Joseph's protection and provision. They have bowed in honor to him, and he used his position to bless them.

Joseph could never have gotten to Pharaoh's palace from Palestine or even Potiphar's house, only from prison where his good attitude and work ethic resulted in his being promoted to assistant jailer while he was still an inmate. He knew the other inmates well enough to recognize sadness on the face of the cupbearer, and cared enough to ask him what was wrong. It is a credit to the cupbearer's trust in Joseph that he asked him to interpret his dreams. Joseph would not have been in the position to save his own family, including the ones who betrayed him, unless he had consistently chosen to have a positive attitude and treated other people with respect and integrity, even when they mistreated him. He did not allow himself to become bitter and start treating others like they had treated him. He chose to be who God called him to be, not who his enemies said he was.

Burns writes, "Joseph was not completely aware of God's plan during the time he was being prepared for the throne. Joseph didn't receive the confirmation of his dreams until his brothers came looking for food a decade later."[40] God never promised to give us the "big picture" so we could find peace in all situations; he promised he would be with us so that we could find peace in all situations. Joseph's faithfulness when he did not understand God's plan gave him victory.

God will sometimes allow difficult or painful situations to prepare us for what is to come; how we handle our pain has a huge impact on the power our suffering has over our recovery. No maneuvering or plotting on Joseph's part could have given him one-tenth of what God gave him. What if Joseph had given in to Potiphar's wife as the one comfort he had in his slavery? Suppose he had responded to his unjust imprisonment with resentfulness and bitterness, and the jailer had seen him as nothing more than another prisoner with a bad attitude? Suppose he had concentrated on his own problems so much that he never noticed that the cupbearer had a long face the morning after his dream? Suppose he had harbored his unforgiveness toward his brothers and had them executed the minute they showed up wanting food? He could easily have manipulated extra rations or comforts for himself in Potiphar's house or the jail, but his honesty and integrity gave him far more. His faithfulness in small things allowed him to receive blessings in much bigger ones. His desire to obey God overwhelmed his desire for self-pity or revenge, and God blessed that obedience abundantly. Joseph knew God well enough to focus past the heartache, to trust despite the circumstances, and expect God to bring his ultimate good. He was able to look for and see God's provisions and blessing, rather than just the hardship and unfairness of his current problems.

His earlier dream came true; they bowed to him...God is always faithful to his promises, but often not in the timing we expect. In Joseph's dream he had respect, position, acclaim, comfort and prestige. Those did come to him, but only after he obediently responded to hatred, abuse, slavery, humiliation, hardship, and betrayal.

He consistently cooperated with those in authority over him in such a way that he won their trust and respect, even during the darkest days of his life. He began as Potiphar's slave; he ended up as Potiphar's boss.

Joseph's "problems" were key to his being in a position to help. He took what he learned during the hard times and chose to use it to better himself, rather than allowing it to fester into unforgiveness that would trap him in self-righteous indignation and resentment. He was trusted by Potiphar, the jailer, the other prisoners, and later even Pharaoh himself. And because he chose to be obedient, even in the face of betrayal, God blessed him and made him prosper, regardless of his circumstances.

The twists and turns in the path of our lives may not make sense until we can view them from a different perspective than our immediate circumstances afford us. We worship and serve God who knows our future – even when that future includes periods of slavery or drought. When we focus on problems and injustice that we cannot control, we may very well lose sight of God. Joseph chose to never stop obeying God, and God worked all that happened to him for his good. God wove all the seemingly unrelated details together into a perfect whole that brought victory and healing in ways none of them could have imagined.

Chuck Swindoll writes, "Pain properly handled can shape a life for greatness".[41] There is absolutely no question that Joseph knew deep pain. But he didn't allow that pain to destroy or diminish him; he "properly handled" it so that it made him stronger. How he handled his pain put him in position to be used by God to save countless people from starvation, and to know the blessing of living among and truly belonging to family again. How you handle your pain will determine whether you are destroyed by it or shaped for greatness.

When Jacob died, all the brothers took his body back to Palestine to bury him. The older brothers feared that Joseph had only been kind to them because of their father. Now that Jacob was dead, they feared that Joseph would take revenge. They sent word to Joseph that their father had asked Joseph to forgive the brothers. Then they came to Joseph and bowed down to him again, offering themselves as his slaves in exchange for their lives. They have spent every day since they sold him, expecting punishment.

Gen 50:19-21 But Joseph said to them, "Don't be afraid. Am I in the place of God? You intended to harm me, but God intended it for good to accomplish what is now being done, the saving of many lives. So then, don't be afraid. I will provide for you and your children." And he reassured them and spoke kindly to them.

Joseph allowed what he knew about God to determine how he responded to betrayal and unfairness. He chose to have hope and be kind and forgiving, rather than give in to self-pity and despair and malice. He knew that vengeance belongs only to God, and he made the intentional choice to be defined by God, rather than by those who opposed him. He did not allow his past to trap him into unforgiveness that would rob him of the future God planned for him. Forgiveness set him free to move forward and become more than he could have ever "asked or imagined". (Eph 3:20) May we do the same.

Rom 8:28 And we know that in all things God works for the good of those who love him, who have been called according to his purpose.

Hosea

Hosea is the only book in the Bible that gives us a glimpse of God's pain as a result of our behavior. Each of the prophets received a specific call to speak God's truth to his people. Some preached instruction; others warned of the consequences of sin. This book of the Bible, Hosea's story, gives us a unique glimpse into the broken heart of God.

Some things just can't be understood until you have experienced them. You can feel compassion or concern, but deep pain is so much bigger than words can convey. Betrayal can cause that kind of pain. God's pain at the betrayal of the people he loved was so deep, was so profound that he singled out Hosea to experience that pain so he could communicate that pain and its consequences to God's people. God not only asked Hosea to love a woman who would betray him; God asked him to continue to love her, even after the betrayal.

It was not unusual for God to direct his prophets to use dramatic means to manifest their message. Isaiah dressed as a prisoner of war for several years to help the people understand that they would be held captive (Is 20:1-3); Jeremiah wore a yoke on his shoulders to warn the people that they would serve others. (Jer 27) Ezekiel also received and odd command.

Ez 3:1-4 And he said to me, "Son of man, eat what is before you, eat this scroll; then go and speak to the house of Israel." So I opened my mouth, and he gave me the scroll to eat. Then he said to me, "Son of man, eat this scroll I am giving you and fill your stomach with it." So I ate it, and it tasted as sweet as honey in my mouth. He then said to me: "Son of man, go now to the house of Israel and speak my words to them."

God asked Ezekiel to consume his word so that he could teach it to the people of Israel. But Hosea had what is probably the most dramatic, painful role of them all. God wanted him to marry a prostitute so that he would be able to convey what God felt when his people rejected him and served other gods. God didn't just want to communicate his Word to them; he asked Hosea to communicate his pain to them.

All we know about Hosea is that he was the son of Beeri and that he lived in the northern kingdom about the same time Isaiah and Amos lived in the southern kingdom. Hosea used many farming references in his writing, but the complexity of his writing style and extensive vocabulary indicate that he was most likely very well educated.

The first three chapters of the book of Hosea tell the story of the prostitute named Gomer. No details of her past are provided. Prostitution in that time was very common and could have been her choice, or she could have been sold into prostitution to pay off a family debt. It was also common for girls to be given as an offering to the Temple of Baal which provided prostitutes for worshippers. Girls would often serve as temple prostitutes for several years and then be released by the priests to marry and have families. Whatever the origin of her prostitution, it was definitely her choice as an adult.

Hos 1:2-3a When the LORD began to speak through Hosea, the LORD said to him, "Go, take to yourself an adulterous wife and children of unfaithfulness, because the land is guilty of the vilest adultery in departing from the LORD." So he married Gomer daughter of Diblaim.

What did Hosea give up when he obeyed God and married her? He had to have known that his wife would never be accepted by the women of his town. He would never know how many of the men of that same town had slept with his wife before he did. He would become the subject of gossip – what kind of a prophet marries a prostitute? Whatever his standing in his community, marrying Gomer would have diminished his reputation and his credibility.

I'm curious as to why Hosea chose this particular prostitute. Did he know her before God's call? Was she a childhood friend? A neighbor? Was he in secretly in love with her and ashamed to marry her? Or did God lead him to a total stranger? Whatever the circumstances, Hosea obeyed.

Chapter two of Hosea indicates that she was not faithful to him while they were married and that she conceived three children in disgrace. (Hos 2:5-9) By chapter three she has left home and returned to prostitution. But this time things deteriorate even further, and she ends up being sold as a slave.

We do not know the details of her return to prostitution. Did Hosea come home one day and just find that Gomer had moved out? Did she still come back to Hosea and her children in the wee hours of the morning? Is that how he knew something was wrong, because she didn't come home one night? Did Hosea spend the time waiting for her to come home feeling anger? Was that anger directed at Gomer or at God? Was he afraid for her? Did he weep? Were his tears for himself or for her? How did he learn she was to be sold at auction? Did someone come and tell him? Were they kind, or did they taunt Hosea with the truth? Or did he go out looking for her? Whatever the circumstances or emotions, God's next command to Hosea was utterly shocking.

Hos 3:1 The LORD said to me, "Go, show your love to your wife again, though she is loved by another and is an adulteress. Love her as the LORD loves the Israelites."

Notice that God did not say, "Bring her home and give her what she needs to survive." He did not say, "Be a good example to her, but never allow her to get close enough to hurt you again." God told Hosea to show love to her, to love her as God loves his people. Going through insincere motions would not demonstrate the love of God. God doesn't love us until we disappoint him or until we betray our relationship with him and then abandon us to what we deserve; he loves us so much that his love never fails to seek us and lead us back to where we belong. He promised us his presence, and that promise is not based on how well we behave; it is based on the unfailing love of God who cannot abandon his people.

In incredible obedience, Hosea went to find Gomer. She had rejected him, and he had to bring her back from somewhere she should never have gone. In that time female slaves were typically sold for thirty shekels of silver and some grain. Hosea bought Gomer for fifteen shekels. This bargain price may have been because she was old or diseased, or maybe they took pity on this shamed husband. Hosea originally made the marriage covenant with her; now he has to buy her redemption from slavery.

God made it very clear that Hosea's obedience was not predicated on Gomer's behavior. Hosea extended acceptance and grace to Gomer that she disdained. He married her with good intentions and expectations, and she betrayed his love. He honored her as his wife, and she refused to honor him as her husband. God commanded that Hosea respond to Gomer's betrayal, not as she deserved, but in keeping with the character of God. In her absence, he has managed his home without her; in taking her back, he extended mercy and authority in their home to her, and made himself vulnerable to her choices once again.

God commanded that Hosea love Gomer, not in spite of what she had done, but for who she could be…the same way he loves us. God does not give up on us when we walk away from him and return to the self-destructive sins that separate us from him. God loves us…even when we betray him. He sent his son to redeem us and bring us back into relationship with him, back to the place and home he has prepared for us.

Hosea's ministry was to call the people of God back into relationship with him. The rest of the book of Hosea gives an account of the betrayal of the people toward God and includes the content of several of Hosea's sermons. As he pleaded with them to repent and return to God, I suspect his voice broke when he compared the Hebrews to common harlots. When he spoke of God's great love for them, despite their betrayal, I cannot imagine he did so without tears. He understood God's pain as he delivered God's message. But he also understood the desire of God's heart and the price of God's promise to forgive and restore that relationship. God refused to give up on his people, and God commanded Hosea not to give up on Gomer.

Hos 2:14-16 "Therefore I am now going to allure her; I will lead her into the desert and speak tenderly to her. There I will give her back her vineyards, and will make the Valley of Achor a door of hope. There she will sing as in the days of her youth, as in the day she came up out of Egypt. In that day," declares the LORD, "you will call me 'my husband'; you will no longer call me 'my master'."

When God's people began to worship other gods and idols, when they ignored his laws and began to trust themselves for the power and prosperity God's blessings had given them, they betrayed God's faithfulness to them. God sent prophets to call them back into relationship with him. Over and over he rescued them from their enemies. He delivered them from slavery and brought them home from captivity. But he would not force them to love him. He chose to risk the pain of betrayal in order to maintain the relationship. God offered forgiveness each time his people asked, and restored them as his precious children every time they chose to honor him as their God. He still does…every time we ask.

God called Hosea to love the unfaithful and forgive the betrayer, just like God loves and forgives us. Our sinful behavior separates us from God just as surely as Gomer's choices separated her from Hosea. If Hosea had treated Gomer as she deserved, she would have received punishment, not mercy. God never excused Gomer's behavior; nor did he allow Hosea to harbor unforgiveness. Hosea was asked to demonstrate God's desire to show us mercy as he offers us forgiveness.

The damage done by betrayal can be far greater than the betrayal itself. Our response to that betrayal can allow us to move past it or to stay trapped in the anger and pain of the event. We can forgive our betrayers and entrust them and our healing to God, or we can harbor unforgiveness and continue to allow their betrayal to cause control our emotions and behavior.

Our relationship with God is tied into our forgiveness of those around us. God wanted Hosea to forgive her so that she could have another chance to repent, and so that Hosea would not be bound to the anger and pain that comes with harboring unforgiveness.

Matt 6:12 Forgive us our debts, as we also have forgiven our debtors.

There is a wonderful quote that has been used by so many that I was unable to find its original source. "Unforgiveness is like drinking poison and expecting the other person to die." Harboring unforgiveness, even when it is very justifiable, hurts no one but the one who refuses to let it go. Elbert Hubbard, an early 20th century author wrote, "The final proof of greatness lies in being able to endure contemptuous treatment without resentment." Whatever your definition of greatness, it cannot include serving the resentment of your past. Neither Joseph nor Hosea allowed betrayal to keep them from God's call on their life. Neither of them indulged their desire for vengeance or getting even. They chose to obey and forgive, even in unfair and painful circumstances. They trusted God to handle the details of the past and the promise of all that was to come. They chose obedience regardless of what others chose. Joseph forgave others, and God showed him his power over the actions of others. God used Hosea to make his people understand how very much he loves us and that even betrayal is not beyond his ability to forgive. Both chose costly obedience that was not based on the pain of the betrayal, but on the love of their God and their belief in his power to redeem what has been into what can be.

Forgiveness in the face of betrayal does not guarantee that you will get your way. Joseph was reunited with his family and his "dreams" came true. There is no indication in the Bible that Hosea's "happily ever after" was ever fulfilled in his marriage. But his faithfulness indicated that he continued to trust God for whatever was to come, regardless of the pain of his current circumstances.

God never calls us to bow down to the abuse others may show us; nor does he want us bound to that abuse. Betrayal will sometimes end a relationship, but it will always change a relationship. Sometimes you need to forgive and restore the relationship; sometimes you need to forgive and move away from the relationship. Always you need to forgive. John MacArthur reminds us that choosing to forgive and entrust your pain and your enemies to God "won't take our trials away, but it will enable us to find joy and peace in the midst of them."[42]

As I was writing this chapter, someone posted this on Facebook. "Forgiveness doesn't excuse their behavior. Forgiveness prevents their behavior from destroying your heart."

Joseph's brothers had to answer for their lies, deceit and treachery, but Joseph's forgiveness released him from the burden of defining himself with their behavior. Hosea's forgiveness of Gomer did not atone for her sin, but it did keep him from disobedience. God's forgiveness of all the ways we betray him each day does not excuse our sin. God commands that we confess our sins and repent, and when we do, his forgiveness keeps us from being trapped in the past. He is willing to "buy us back", to redeem us, and give us a new future and hope.

The need to forgive does not diminish the depth of your pain. Your forgiveness does not excuse those who have betrayed you – they must handle that with God for themselves. But your forgiveness ends their ability to control your anger and resentment and bitterness, to keep you captive to what has been. It frees you to move forward without that burden.

What if God desires that your forgiveness serve as his conduit to pour his mercy and love in the life of the one who has betrayed you? What if your forgiveness is the way God chooses to draw your betrayer back into relationship with him? What if your ability to forgive them is the required step toward what God wants next for your life? Whether or not your forgiveness includes restoration of the relationship, it allows you to move forward in obedience, unshackled to the one who brought you pain.

Those who betrayed you may have wounded you deeply. God wants to heal that wound, but your healing must begin with forgiveness. May we never give those who have hurt us the power to keep us from God's presence and blessings. When you refuse to continue to serve the one who betrayed you, you are set free to serve only God…and he loves you more than you can ask or imagine.

Chapter 6

People like you who were heartbroken and struggle to let go of their pain

Our hearts can break for any number of reasons, at any stage of our lives. There is real pain when we get cut from the team or lose an important game. Someone else may get the part or promotion that we worked hard to achieve. We can lose hope in a dream, or miss an incredible opportunity. We can be rejected by one we want a relationship with or we can lose one we love in death. The idea of losing something we fervently wanted to have or to keep is integral to heartbreak. Heartbreak can change our expectations, our future, our self-definition, or our choices, but heartbreak always changes us.

Some respond to heartbreak with anger and rejection. Others respond by isolating themselves and avoiding any situations that could reproduce that pain. It is easier to be angry than to grieve. It is easier to put on a façade and try to convince the world that we are fine than it is to handle our pain in public. Whether our broken heart manifests itself as loneliness or gives us an inability to move forward, real heartbreak always leaves a scar.

A truly broken heart cannot be explained with a definition or analyzed with a formula. It is beyond explanation and is felt in the deepest, most vulnerable places that words cannot touch. The concept of "break" is integral to what happens. Our expectations, our perspective, our priorities, our dreams are suddenly broken. Things that are broken don't work correctly....and when we are broken by grief and pain, neither do we.

Ignoring brokenness will not allow it to heal in such a way that it is useful again. Breaks in bones and in skin leave scars. We can have a doctor set the bone or stitch a deep wound in such a way that it eventually is not even noticeable, but ignoring it or pathetically trying to "patch" it ourselves will usually result in loss of motion, a limp, or visible scars. Broken hearts work much the same way. Clinging to broken pieces of our lives and dreams will not magically reassemble them. While each one of us grieves differently, we have to intentionally handle the broken things in our lives. We can make a willful choice to try to rebuild what we used to have, to use the broken pieces to build something new, or we can be trapped by the broken pieces that we refuse to release.

What do you do with your pain when your plans don't work out? Are you more interested in protecting your pain or in moving past it toward what is ahead? Will your brokenness drive you toward God or will it leave you isolated with your pain? Will you trust him to continue to be who he has always been, or will you seek your security somewhere else?

Mary Magdalen

Luke 8:1-3 After this, Jesus traveled about from one town and village to another, proclaiming the good news of the kingdom of God. The Twelve were with him, and also some women who had been cured of evil spirits and diseases: Mary (called Magdalen) from whom seven demons had come out; Joanna the wife of Cuza, the manager of Herod's household; Susanna; and many others. These women were helping to support them out of their own means.

Mary Magdalen entered biblical account as a part of a group. She was just one of the ones who followed Jesus from town to town. While many commonly assume she is a prostitute, there is no evidence that is true. We know that in that time they often explained medical and psychological problems as demons, and we have no idea what hers were. Did they manifest themselves as mental illness like depression or rage or confusion? Was she delusional? Did she have an inexplicable illness like epilepsy or narcolepsy? All we know is that those seven demons were no match for

Jesus who healed her from them. Her response to that healing was to follow the one who had set her free.

Because gospel accounts mostly provide stories of Jesus' interaction with the disciples, we do not really know much about her during Jesus' ministry. What miracles did she witness? What teaching did she hear? Everything about her had changed; she was no longer ruled by her demons. Jesus gave her new hope and purpose. There is no specific evidence that she was singled out like Peter, James, and John. She apparently did not make trouble or headlines; she just stayed with those who stayed with Jesus...until they abandoned him and she didn't.

John 19:25 Near the cross of Jesus stood his mother, his mother's sister, Mary the wife of Clopas, and Mary Magdalen. When Jesus saw his mother there, and the disciple whom he loved standing nearby, he said to his mother, "Dear woman, here is your son," and to the disciple, "Here is your mother." From that time on, this disciple took her into his home.

When you consider this passage from Mary Magdalen's point of view, she seems so very alone. Jesus' mother had her sister, and Jesus gave her to John who would care for her for the rest of her life. The other Mary had a husband named Clopas. Mary Magdalen was the only one who didn't belong to anyone. She has followed the one who saved her from the demons that threatened to destroy her, and now her worst nightmare is in progress. She heard the nails being driven in, Jesus' last words, and the soldiers' mocking taunts. She watched him writhe in pain and the soldiers gamble for his robe; she watched blood drip from his body and the color fade from his face. She was both horrified and heartbroken by the hypocrisy and evil that was separating her from the one who had loved her enough to save her. She saw the darkness and felt the earthquake. Everything that she had become, everything that she hoped for was dying on a cross, shamefully condemned. And she was alone.

Matt 27:55-61 Many women were there, watching from a distance. They had followed Jesus from Galilee to care for his needs. Among them were Mary Magdalen, Mary the mother of James and Joses, and the mother of Zebedee's sons. As evening approached, there came a rich man from Arimathea, named Joseph, who had himself become a disciple of Jesus. Going to Pilate, he asked for Jesus' body, and Pilate ordered that it be given to him. Joseph took the body, wrapped it in a clean linen cloth, and placed it in his own new tomb that he had cut out of the rock. He rolled a big stone in front of the entrance to the tomb and went away. Mary Magdalen and the other Mary were sitting there opposite the tomb.

Sabbath would start at sundown. Jesus had to be buried quickly. Sabbath law required that the burial had to be done before sundown or wait until after Sabbath. Mark 15:43 describes Joseph of Arimathea as a "prominent member of the Council". He puts his professional reputation on the line to provide a new tomb to hold the dead body of Jesus. He sealed the tomb and went away, leaving Mary Magdalen and the other Mary alone at the tomb. How long did they sit there? Were they hysterical with grief or numb with shock? Did they pray or were they speechless? Did they ask God for mercy or did they fear that their faith had been in vain? How long before they went "home"? Since they came to Jerusalem for Passover, that "home" may have looked far more like a campsite than a house. Did they know how to find the scattered disciples, or were they alone for that awful Sabbath?

Mark 16:1-4 When the Sabbath was over, Mary Magdalen, Mary the mother of James, and Salome bought spices so that they might go to anoint Jesus' body. Very early on the first day of the week, just after sunrise, they were on their way to the tomb and they asked each other, "Who will roll the stone away from the entrance of the tomb?" But when they looked up, they saw that the stone, which was very large, had been rolled away.

I absolutely believe there is not one insignificant detail in God's Word. There was no rush that first Easter morning. They had seen Jesus' dead body. Sleeping in just a bit after this horrific couple of days may have been just what they needed. But it is not what they did. They went "very early... just after sunrise." Was it because they could not sleep? Did Mary spend a sleepless night, watching for signs of daylight so that she could go and serve Jesus one last time? All that remains of her salvation and hopes and dreams is a dead body lying in a tomb, and caring for that body is the only way she has of dealing with her pain.

Mary Magdalen's story here reminds me of the account of a young, Christian mother who stood beside the casket of her five year old son. One who beheld her immense grief reminded her that her son wasn't in that casket. The mother replied, "I know that his soul is in heaven…but this is the hair I brushed, this is the hand I held; I have put band aids on those knees and kisses on those cheeks. This body is precious to me. It is all I have left of him right now." Jesus' body was all Mary Magdalen had left of her Savior and her dreams.

When the women arrived at the tomb, the stone had been rolled back from the entrance. Jesus conquered death and came back to life. Shifting a stone would not have been much of a challenge after that. Besides, Jesus will appear later that day behind a locked door. The stone was not rolled away to let Jesus out of the tomb; it was rolled away to let those who loved Jesus into the tomb.

Mark 16:5-8 As they entered the tomb, they saw a young man dressed in a white robe sitting on the right side, and they were alarmed. "Don't be alarmed," he said. "You are looking for Jesus the Nazarene, who was crucified. He has risen! He is not here. See the place where they laid him. But go, tell his disciples and Peter, 'He is going ahead of you into Galilee. There you will see him, just as he told you'." Trembling and bewildered, the women went out and fled from the tomb.

John 20:1-8 Early on the first day of the week, while it was still dark, Mary Magdalen went to the tomb and saw that the stone had been removed from the entrance. So she came running to Simon Peter and the other disciple, the one Jesus loved, and said, "They have taken the Lord out of the tomb, and we don't know where they have put him!" So Peter and the other disciple started for the tomb. Both were running, but the other disciple outran Peter and reached the tomb first. He bent over and looked in at the strips of linen lying there but did not go in. Then Simon Peter, who was behind him, arrived and went into the tomb. He saw the strips of linen lying there, as well as the burial cloth that had been around Jesus' head. The cloth was folded up by itself, separate from the linen. Finally the other disciple, who had reached the tomb first, also went inside. He saw and believed.

When the women told the disciples, Peter and John ran for the tomb to see for themselves. (Any parent who has raised boys has to smile at John's account when he tells that both he and Peter ran for the tomb, but John got there first....that competitive spirit is as old as time.) Once they had seen for themselves, the disciples went back to where they felt safer, but Mary Magdalen refused to leave.

John 20:10-13 Then the disciples went back to their homes, but Mary stood outside the tomb crying. As she wept, she bent over to look into the tomb and saw two angels in white, seated where Jesus' body had been, one at the head and the other at the foot. They asked her, "Woman, why are you crying?" "They have taken my Lord away," she said, "and I don't know where they have put him."

I am fascinated that Peter and John did not see the angels, but Mary Magdalen did. Why didn't the angels speak to the disciples as well? Notice her tenacity. She is so focused on finding Jesus' body, she doesn't even question the appearance of the angels. She doesn't demand to know why these have entered the tomb of her savior. She doesn't bow in recognition the she is in the presence of holy messengers. They acknowledge her tears, but she barely acknowledges their presence. She just wants to find the body of her Lord so that she can do the only thing she knows to do for him.

John 20:14-18 At this, she turned around and saw Jesus standing there, but she did not realize that it was Jesus. "Woman," he said, "why are you crying? Who is it you are looking for?" Thinking he was the gardener, she said, "Sir, if you have carried him away, tell me where you have put him, and I will get him." Jesus said to her, "Mary." She turned toward him and cried out in Aramaic, "Rabboni!" (which means Teacher). Jesus said, "Do not hold on to me, for I have not yet returned to the Father. Go instead to my brothers and tell them, 'I am returning to my Father and your Father, to my God and your God'." Magdalen went to the disciples with the news: "I have seen the Lord!" And she told them that he had said these things to her.

Those two men robed in white in the tomb did not give her any help, so she tried her luck with this guy. She assumes he is the gardener. Who else would be there at that time of day? He addressed her as "woman" and asks why she is crying. Again she gives her story. I love the fact that she thinks she will be able to carry the dead body. Wonder where she planned to take him? Back to the same tomb that didn't hold him the first go round? Does she have a Plan B in mind? Why doesn't she recognize that the one standing before her is the one she is desperately trying to find?

The verb here for crying is actually better translated "every demonstration of grief". This is not a few lonely tears trickling down her cheek; this is a falling apart kind of heartbreak that is taking over. She made it to the tomb, but the disappearance of his body is more than she could bear. Do her tears blur her vision? Is she so focused on her pain that she cannot recognize the answer? Women in that day did not look a strange man in the eye. Was she bowed by ritual of her culture or falling back into the shame of her past when she was outcast because of her seven demons? Was part of her grief the loss, not only of her Savior, but of the one who had given her a new chance, new self-esteem...that she lost again when Jesus died?

And Jesus spoke her name. Wouldn't you love to have heard his tone of voice? Was his voice choked at the sight of her tears? Did it reflect tenderness in the face of her grief? Was it soothing? Joyful?

It seems to me that narrative is left out of this part of the story. She recognizes him as "Teacher" and then the story skips to his warning her "don't hang on to me". I suspect that she probably went flying to grasp that body that she had come to honor. She came to anoint his dead body, and found herself clutching his resurrected body.

"Don't hang on to me." Maybe he just wants her to back up and let him see her face. Maybe her enthusiasm is getting in the way of her understanding. Maybe he is preparing her for when he will leave her and send the Holy Spirit to her.

The first person Christ appeared to after his Resurrection was the one who refused to let him go. Our broken hearts can only be healed when we offer them back to God. God never promised to protect us from heartbreak, but he does promise us his presence in it and to bring good from it. Mary Magdalen's first encounter with Christ changed her forever; so did this one. What she experienced that first Easter morning is the Easter moment we all need. We all need to hear God speak our name. We need to recognize that he is capable of giving us new hope and new dreams that we cannot even imagine as we trust him with the broken pieces of our present.

Thomas

Thomas has gotten a bad "rap" in church teaching. My irritation with those who dismiss Thomas by perpetually identifying him as "Doubting Thomas" is the reason I originally began writing this book. Jesus did acknowledge doubt in Thomas' life; he also acknowledges it in Peter's life. Peter didn't get the nickname, "Doubting Peter"; why saddle Thomas with it?

Matt 14:30-31 But when he [Peter] saw the wind, he was afraid and, beginning to sink, cried out, "Lord, save me!" Immediately Jesus reached out his hand and caught him. "You of little faith," he said, "why did you doubt?"

Doubt is usually a secondary emotion expressed typically "when we feel uncomfortable with the expression of a primary emotion".[43] Peter's primary emotion was almost certainly fear, and his response to his fear was to respond to imminent threat with doubt about his immediate future. It is dangerous to take one detail and try to make it the whole story. Identifying Thomas as "Doubting Thomas" requires us to ignore much more compelling evidence of his character. He may have momentarily doubted the Resurrection, but I am absolutely convinced that his hesitation came from a broken heart, not from disbelief. He, like Peter, choose to express the secondary emotion of doubt, rather than deal with the primary emotion of grief.

All four gospels specifically mention that Jesus calls Thomas as a disciple. Thomas is usually referred to as "the twin". (Makes me wonder… were he and his twin close? Were they identical? How did the twin feel about Thomas just taking off with some itinerant preacher?) Peter, James and John frequently get the top billing as disciples singled out by Jesus. (I wonder if that is because they were particularly close to Jesus, or if they just needed extra supervision?) Thomas is not in that "inner circle". My guess is that Thomas was an introvert. Biblical evidence indicates he was not afraid to ask questions and that he was passionate about his beliefs. We are given important insight into Thomas' character on two specific occasions while Jesus was preparing the disciples to carry on after his death....before they knew he was going to die without establishing an earthly kingdom.

At the end of John 10 we learn that Jesus has seriously irritated the Jewish authorities, and just barely gotten away from them before heading back to the Jordan – a safe distance away from Jerusalem. Then, from that position of relative safety, Jesus suddenly announces that he is going right back to the place where they want him dead.

> John 11:1-16 Now a man named Lazarus was sick. He was from Bethany, the village of Mary and her sister Martha. This Mary, whose brother Lazarus now lay sick, was the same one who poured perfume on the Lord and wiped his feet with her hair. So the sisters sent word to Jesus, "Lord, the one you love is sick." When he heard this, Jesus said, "This sickness will not end in death. No, it is for God's glory so that God's Son may be glorified through it." Jesus loved Martha and her sister and Lazarus. Yet when he heard that Lazarus was sick, he stayed where he was two more days. Then he said to his disciples, "Let us go back to Judea." "But Rabbi," they said, "a short while ago the Jews tried to stone you, and yet you are going back there?" Jesus answered, "Are there not twelve hours of daylight? A man who walks by day will not stumble, for he sees by this world's light. It is when he walks by night that he stumbles, for he has no light." After he had said this, he went on to tell them, "Our friend Lazarus has fallen asleep; but I am going there to wake him up." His disciples replied, "Lord, if he sleeps, he will get better." Jesus had been speaking of his death, but his disciples thought he meant natural sleep. So then he told them plainly, "Lazarus is dead, and for your sake I am glad I was not there, so that you may believe. But let us go to him." Then Thomas (called Didymus) said to the rest of the disciples, "Let us also go, that we may die with him."

Bethany is about two miles from Jerusalem. The disciples know that they are relatively safe at the Jordan, but Bethany is well within the reach of the authorities. Once the people who "tried to seize" Jesus in John

10:39 found out he was close, they might actually succeed this time, and they might include the disciples, as well. When Thomas realized that Jesus would not be dissuaded from going to Bethany, his response was very telling. He would rather go with Jesus and face his own death, than hide in safety without Jesus.

Thomas' other pre-Resurrection defining moment also illustrates his fervent desire not to be separated from Jesus. Jesus fervently loves these twelve with whom he has spent the last three years, and he knows how very difficult the coming events will be for them. He tries to make them understand that they will be separated from him and tries to mitigate it with his tender, powerful promise of eternity:

John 14:1-6 "Do not let your hearts be troubled. You believe in God; believe also in me. My Father's house has many rooms; if that were not so, would I have told you that I am going there to prepare a place for you? And if I go and prepare a place for you, I will come back and take you to be with me that you also may be where I am. You know the way to the place where I am going." Thomas said to him, "Lord, we don't know where you are going, so how can we know the way?" Jesus answered, "I am the way and the truth and the life. No one comes to the Father except through me."

Thomas does not want understanding or comfort; he wants a roadmap with a guarantee. He wants assurance that he will be able to find Jesus, that he won't be separated from him for long. In both these accounts you see a fierce determination in Thomas to stay close to Jesus. He will face death and follow him anywhere, but he will not be separated from him.

And then comes the unthinkable. Jesus, the Son of God, washed Thomas' feet. They sang hymns together before going to the olive grove at Gethsemane to pray. Thomas undoubtedly watched as the soldiers came to arrest Jesus. He saw Judas betray Jesus with a kiss, and Peter cut off the ear of the servant to the High Priest. He watched Jesus perform one last miracle by reattaching that ear. And then his worst fears were realized.

One Sunday morning during worship, my pastor read a verse that I'd never seen before.

Luke 23:49 But all those who knew him, including the women who had followed him from Galilee, stood at a distance, watching these things.

"All those who knew him". There is so much in that verse that is not said. How big of a distance? What "these things" were included in what they saw? Did they hear the crowds condemn Christ and ask for the life of Barabbas? Did they see the soldiers beat Jesus until he was almost unrecognizable? Were any of them along the path that led Jesus to Golgotha? Were they close enough to hear the soldiers nail Jesus to the cross? Did they experience the earthquake and darkness? Did they see them remove his body from the cross and take it away to be buried? Were the disciples all together? In small groups?

The only two disciples for whom we have any information during this time period are Peter and John. We know that Peter was in the courtyard during Jesus' trial, and we know that John was with Jesus' mother and at least two other women at the foot of Jesus' cross. Where was Thomas? Where did he spend that next few days? All the disciples scatter in fear; all are undoubtedly heartbroken and terrified at this horrifying turn of events. But by Sunday night they are all back together, except for two. Only Thomas and Judas are not with the others that Easter Sunday night. Judas had committed suicide, but we have no idea where Thomas was. The other ten have heard the reports of the women from the tomb; Peter and John confirmed their stories, but they were all hiding behind a locked door that Sunday night when Jesus showed up in their midst. They grieved for three days before Jesus came to find them. They saw him and heard him. They knew that Jesus was back from the dead, and their faith is reborn.

But Thomas didn't see, didn't hear. Why wasn't he with them? Where would he have been? Why was he the only one that did not seek the others? Was his grief so deep that he could not bear to be with people who reminded him that he had lost the one person he didn't want to lose? He must have wondered how he could have been so sure of the truth, and so wrong. Why did he finally rejoin them? When they tell him that they've seen Christ, he either can't or won't believe them.

John 20:24-25 Now Thomas (called Didymus), one of the Twelve, was not with the disciples when Jesus came. So the other disciples told him, "We have seen the Lord!" But he said to them, "Unless I see the nail marks in his hands and put my finger where the nails were, and put my hand into his side, I will not believe it."

Thomas doesn't accuse them of lying; he simply says he refuses to believe. His response here smacks of anger that covers incredible pain. His heart was shattered when he lost, not only his friend, but his hope for the future, the confidence that God had a plan to save his people. On Friday night, it appeared that evil had won, and that all Thomas had believed was false. His pain was so immense that his self-defense quickly built a wall that would prevent that kind of pain from ever destroying him again. He could not allow himself to ever trust like that again. Hearing their stories did not alleviate his pain; second hand accounts will not sustain our faith in heartbreak. We need a personal encounter to take away our pain.

I firmly believe that Thomas' response to Jesus' death was rooted in a completely broken heart. He had dedicated the last three years of his life to being in the presence of his Lord; then his Lord died. Thomas' dreams and expectations were destroyed on a cross. He had been ready to die with Jesus, but Jesus died without him.

An entire week passed. Thomas was not with the disciples when Jesus first showed up; Thomas had an entire extra week to grieve without hope. He chose to isolate himself from them at the beginning of the horrors that followed the arrest, and suffered needlessly for an extra week. Isolation does that. It may give us temporary respite from our pain, but it alienates us from what can strengthen and heal us, as well.

We have no narrative from that week, but the next time Jesus appeared to the disciples, Thomas was with them. Did he finally go to them, or did one of them go find him? Wonder why he stayed with people who told him what he refused to believe? Were they tender with Thomas' pain, or did they just give him "space"? Wonder if they talked about their favorite "Jesus" moments? If they just sat silently, finding comfort in the presence of others who had loved him as well?

John 20:26-28 A week later his disciples were in the house again, and Thomas was with them. Though the doors were locked, Jesus came and stood among them and said, "Peace be with you!" Then he said to Thomas, "Put your finger here; see my hands. Reach out your hand and put it into my side. Stop doubting and believe." Thomas said to him, "My Lord and my God!"

Jesus knew. He knew Thomas hadn't been there. He knew Thomas' pain. He knew exactly what Thomas had said, and repeated it back to him. He did not scold Thomas for his doubt; he did not express disappointment that Thomas hadn't remembered what he had told him; he did not berate Thomas for abandoning him in the garden or for deserting the group on Easter Sunday. Jesus knew what Thomas needed, and Jesus appeared to reassure him, to give him back his hope and his joy. He offered Thomas the physical evidence he needed to get past the pain and doubt, and move on to what was ahead. There is no evidence that Thomas actually touched Christ. Seeing the risen Christ was enough to remind Thomas that Jesus is God, no matter what the circumstances look like. Being in Jesus' presence gave him the hope and courage he needed to recognize that God was doing something new.

I am a dog person. I have owned and dearly loved seven dogs since I was a little girl, and it is my fervent intention never to be without the love and joy of sharing my life with a dog. I believe they are the best example of unconditional love on this earth. I have delighted in sharing my life with them, and grieved deeply when each one of them died. Maybe I have just been blessed to have exceptionally wonderful dogs, but the unconditional love I have known from these dogs and the joy they brought to my life was worth the heartbreak of losing them and every tear I cried when they died.

I have known people who dearly loved their pets as a member of their family, but their response to the pain of losing the pet was that they would never have another one because the pain of the loss was too great to ever face again. Their response to the horrible pain of grief is to make sure they never have to face it again. I believe this self-defense is the best explanation for Thomas' behavior after the Resurrection. Protection from ever having to feel pain can cost us the joy that makes our lives worthwhile. Jesus did not promise that we would never feel pain; he does promise to be present with us when we do.

There are two more glimpses of Thomas in scripture. In both, he is with the disciples. Anyone who has experienced the pain of a deep loss can attest to the fact that there is some serious discomfort in finding a "new normal". The disciples know Jesus has risen from the dead, but their relationship with him is different now. Jesus is not with them all the time; he just shows up every once in a while. The next time we see Thomas is in Capernaum, Peter's hometown. I find it interesting that in this period of "dis-ease", Peter goes home to do what he used to do before he met Jesus. The other disciples just go with him. They go out to fish and spend all night catching nothing. And then, in the mist of the early dawn, they hear a voice from the shore.

John 21:1-9 Afterward Jesus appeared again to his disciples, by the Sea of Tiberias. It happened this way: Simon Peter, Thomas (called Didymus), Nathanael from Cana in Galilee, the sons of Zebedee, and two other disciples were together. "I'm going out to fish," Simon Peter told them, and they said, "We'll go with you." So they went out and got into the boat, but that night they caught nothing. Early in the morning, Jesus stood on the shore, but the disciples did not realize that it was Jesus. He called out to them, "Friends, haven't you any fish?" "No," they answered. He said, "Throw your net on the right side of the boat and you will find some." When they did, they were unable to haul the net in because of the large number of fish. Then the disciple whom Jesus loved said to Peter, "It is the Lord!" As soon as Simon Peter heard him say, "It is the Lord," he wrapped his outer garment around him (for he had taken it off) and jumped into the water. The other disciples followed in the boat, towing the net full of fish, for they were not far from shore, about a hundred yards. When they landed, they saw a fire of burning coals there with fish on it, and some bread.

When their world felt out of control, they went fishing, looking for what had brought them comfort and predictability before…and caught nothing. It is odd to me that they do not recognize or question this voice from the shore. I wonder if Thomas was mad that Peter bailed out and waded ashore, leaving them one less man to row as they towed the huge catch to shore. I wonder if Thomas wanted to run to Jesus and cling to him, or if he was held back by awe and reverence. There is no reference to Jesus speaking to Thomas during this early morning cookout on the beach, but I wonder if he caught Thomas' eye or hugged his shoulder as he served him some fish.

Thomas' heartbreak that separated him from the disciples on Easter morning was gone. In Acts 1:10-14 Thomas was with them as they watched Jesus ascend to heaven and then went to meet with other believers as they tried to figure out what God wanted next. Again, Thomas is separated from Jesus. But this time he understands that the separation is temporary. Jesus had restored his broken heart so that he could move forward with peace into whatever this "new normal" would look like. Jesus left to prepare a place for Thomas…and for each of us. Thomas received the Holy Spirit at Pentecost and served his Lord on earth until his Lord called him home, never to be separated again.

What we do with our broken hearts determines who we become. At a Women of Faith Conference in 2013 Sheila Walsh said, "God can only heal a broken life if you give him all the pieces." Refusing to let go of the pieces of our broken heart leaves us with pieces that do not fit anymore. God can build a new normal, but we have to be willing to let go and allow him to repair, restore, and redeem all that we think we have lost.

We are all broken. Last Sunday I was moved to tears as I looked across the faces gathered in my church on a Sunday morning and remembered their stories. That precious, frail lady has just buried her husband of more than fifty years. That man is unemployed, again, through no fault of his own. That couple has just put their son into a mental institution. That father is trying to keep his son out of jail. That adult caregiver is desperately trying to meet incredible physical needs with no emotional support. That woman has been shattered by a divorce decree that ended a marriage she so wanted to preserve. That teenager is desperately trying to find the line between being loved and ungodly compromise. Everyone one of them brought the wounded, broken pieces of their lives into worship. And those are just the stories I know. God is not intimidated by our broken hearts and dreams; it is in our brokenness that his power is most evident.

Satan will try to convince you that your broken heart exempts you from obedience, that somehow nursing your pain will make it better, that you are too broken to be of any use to God, or that your life ended when your heart broke. He is the Father of Lies. We live in a fallen world that will break our hearts. Trust the one who loves you the most with all the pieces of your brokenness. Bring those pieces into his presence and ask him to rebuild, to heal, to resurrect, to transform what was into what can be. Your life here is not over until he calls you home. Give him all the pieces of your brokenness and trust him to build your "new normal".

Chapter 7

People like you who had regret and struggle to let go of their past

"If only" will almost never happen. There are no real "do-overs" in life; only fresh starts. We all have things in our lives that we wish we had done differently or not done at all, things that have made us question the wisdom of ever trying or trusting again. Sometimes that regret comes from innocent but stupid choices; sometimes from intentional sin. Sometimes we are responsible for our own regret; sometimes our regret comes from the choices of others. But regret always makes us hesitant to move forward as we decide what to do with the "if only" broken plans and dreams of our past. What we wish had happened differently in the past can make our present more painful, and may make us less trusting of God.

Choosing to be controlled by your regret can make you captive to guilt and shame. Focusing on a past that you cannot change will keep you from living in the preset or moving forward to envision a hopeful future. Moving past your regret will require a conscious choice to focus on what is next, rather than what has been. Part of the problem with regret is that we usually have only ourselves to blame, either for what we have or haven't done. We can allow ourselves to be the victim of our choices, or we can start to make new choices.

In his book *AHA: The God Moment That Changes Everything* Kyle Idleman says that "...the number-one contributor to spiritual growth is difficult circumstances."[44] Each of us can look back and feel regret for how we handled or responded to our difficult circumstances, but we also have the power to define ourselves by our comebacks, rather than our losses.

Regret can become a positive motivator when we allow it to move us away from where we don't want to be anymore. Wallowing in futile hopes of "if only" will not change our circumstances; refocusing our emotional energy to "now what?" can initiate the change that will become a fresh start. Idleman identifies three required components to the choice to move us from where we no longer want to be to a fresh start: sudden awakening, brutal honesty, and immediate action.[45] People who take ownership of their poor choices and who are willing to take action to change them find that they have fresh starts that will not erase their past, but will prevent them from being a victim of their own making. Two of the best biblical examples of sudden awakening, brutal honesty, and immediate action are the Prodigal Son and the apostle Paul.

Prodigal Son

While this is a "...parable and not a real-life story, it doesn't mean it isn't a story full of real life. It's almost impossible to read this story without finding yourself in it."[46] I often wonder how many of Jesus' stories are based on real events, and whether those real events particularly resonated with someone in the crowd listening to his story. Even if this young man was not an actual person who was confronted with a choice, it is a parable that Jesus used to illustrate truth about our Father's love for us and to teach us how to respond to our sin. How this young man handled his regret in the story is Jesus' way of teaching us what to do with our own regret.

Luke 15:11-13 There was a man who had two sons. The younger one said to his father, "Father, give me my share of the estate." So he divided his property between them. Not long after that, the younger son got together all he had, set off for a distant country and there squandered his wealth in wild living.

If you have been a young adult or if you have grown children, you know firsthand the dangers of choices made by people who have more confidence than experience or sound judgment. This young man had dreams and plans that were not confined to his father's farm. He wanted to be on his own and experience life as he imagined it could be.

Idleman points out that this son was not just leaving his father; he was leaving the Jewish faith.[47] Most scholars agree that the "distant country" he referred to was most probably an area of ten Gentile cities known at that time as Decapolis to the east and south of the Sea of Galilee. These cities were heavily influenced by Greek philosophy and were characterize by the worship of many gods. Drunkenness, prostitution, and homosexuality were common in many of their religious rituals.[48]

How painful that must have been for the father. The son would have received this share of the inheritance when his father died, but he did not want to wait that long. He wanted his freedom more than he wanted relationship. He wanted his father to give him the money he would use to abandon all that the father valued. He felt entitled to what he had no right to demand. He was arrogant enough to think he deserved what he wanted, that he was smarter than the enemies he would face in the world, and that his inheritance was more important than his family.

Why didn't the father try to talk the boy out of leaving? Why did God give us free will? Instruction in God's word is clear, yet we so often refuse to believe it until we learn it the hard way. What did the father know that the son had to learn in the far country?

As a classroom teacher I watched so many students excuse laziness with the assurance that "grades don't really matter", and then be so very disappointed when their post high school choices were limited. As a parent I watched my children ignore godly counsel and trust people who took advantage of them, who encouraged them to make choices that did not bring their good. As a child of God, I have assumed that I'm the exception, that the rules don't necessarily apply to me, and been filled with regret over the messes I've created for myself. When God's beloved children refuse to obey his instruction, he allows them to learn from the consequences of their choices that break his heart.

Idleman identifies the distant country as "any area of our lives where we are trying to live independently of the Father."[49] We want to walk away from him, ignoring his counsel, taking charge of our own lives. We choose to leave his presence, but expect to take his blessings with us. God's laws for us are not about his need for power; they are from the heart of a Father who knows the evil of our "distant country" and wants to protect us from it.

That son walked away from his father's farm, faith, and protection to what he hoped would be a glorious adventure and the beginning of a new, fulfilling life. "Distant countries" away from our Father are always so attractive in the plans we imagine; temptation wouldn't work if we knew the truth about it.

Luke 15:14-20a After he had spent everything, there was a severe famine in that whole country, and he began to be in need. So he went and hired himself out to a citizen of that country, who sent him to his fields to feed pigs. He longed to fill his stomach with the pods that the pigs were eating, but no one gave him anything. When he came to his senses, he said, "How many of my father's hired men have food to spare, and here I am starving to death! I will set out and go back to my father and say to him: Father, I have sinned against heaven and against you. I am no longer worthy to be called your son; make me like one of your hired men." So he got up and went to his father.

His new start in the distant country did not work out according to plan. What the world had told him about money and independence and fun didn't turn out to be true in his life. The "far country" cost him more than it was worth. Eventually his regret forced him to choose between where he was and where he knew he should be. How long was he there before things went so wrong? Did a girl there break his heart? Was he betrayed by people he trusted? Did they take advantage of him and spend his father's money and then abandon him when the money was gone? To his credit, he didn't go running home as soon as the famine hit and he ran out of money; he found a job. Pork is considered unclean by the Jews. His choice to abandon his father led to his serving what he should have considered unclean. How long did he envy the pigs menu before he decided to leave what he had chosen and return to where he belonged?

"When he came to his senses" is the key phrase in this story. He didn't just recognize the problem and feel sorry for himself. This was his sudden awakening. His brutal honesty about the consequences of his choices led him to take immediate action. We are not told what precipitated this sudden awakening. Was there single event or did discomfort and homesickness just gradually overtake his stubbornness and pride? What has to happen before we "come to our senses"? When do we stop choosing to serve our regret and things that are "unclean" and start making choices that change things for the better? How long do we allow ourselves to be held captive in that far country because we don't want to admit we were wrong? Because our pride thinks we can continue down the wrong path and still end up where we want to go? Why do we insist on learning the hard way?

Idleman tenderly suggests that each of us has our "pigpen moment", and encourages us to examine our answers to the sentence: "I stopped running from God when..."[50] The Prodigal Son stopped running when he preferred telling his Father the truth to going hungry. He began to recognize the home he so eagerly left as the one place he wanted to be.

We will stop running only when we are willing to be honest with ourselves and with our Father, when we are willing to make choices that will change our circumstances. God never intends for us to "come to our senses" and wallow in regret over what has become of our lives; his plan for our lives is to take action that will move us from regret back into relationship with him.

This son did not blame the so-called friends, the famine, or the pig farmer. He was honest with himself and decided to be honest with his father. He chose to take responsibility for his choices and to take action that would precipitate change. After he "came to his senses", he came up with a plan.

Luke 15:18-20a I will set out and go back to my father and say to him: "Father, I have sinned against heaven and against you. I am no longer worthy to be called your son; make me like one of your hired men." So he got up and went to his Father.

Was the pig farmer angry that he had to hire someone else, or did he give the young man provisions for his trip home? Did the son formulate and rehearse this speech in his mind as he walked the long miles back home? Did all of his favorite things about "home" run through his mind on his way back, or did he fear the condemnation and rejection he deserved? As he realized he was almost home, did his steps quicken or slow?

Luke 15:20b-24 But while he was still a long way off, his father saw him and was filled with compassion for him; he ran to his son, threw his arms around him and kissed him. The son said to him, "Father, I have sinned against heaven and against you. I am no longer worthy to be called your son." But the father said to his servants, "Quick! Bring the best robe and put it on him. Put a ring on his finger and sandals on his feet. Bring the fattened calf and kill it. Let's have a feast and celebrate. For this son of mine was dead and is alive again; he was lost and is found." So they began to celebrate.

"While he was still a long way off"…it almost never fails to bring tears to my eyes when I read that phrase. How many nights did that father see the empty place at the table and pray or weep? Oh, how the father must have grieved the absence of a son who had rejected him and broken his heart, who did not deserve his love or the respect of this family; yet the father still scanned the horizon constantly, hoping against hope that his son would return. How far away was that son when the father recognized that profile, that gait?

"He ran to his son". This young man did not deserve his father's love when he left; he did not deserve it when he returned. It was considered undignified for proper Jewish men to run. The father has not even heard the speech or apology yet. When the son actually begins the speech, the father interrupts him before he is finished; he never even hears the part about "make me like one of your hired men". There is no question of his becoming a hired servant. This is his son, and nothing, not even painful choices of the past, will change that.

The father gives him a robe, a ring, and sandals. These clearly indicate that this son has been restored to his father's house. I wonder if the father had kept them handy…just in hope that his son would wear them again one day. This father fervently desires restored relationship. He watches for the return of this son and immediately throws a party to celebrate. They are no longer bound by the sins of the son's past; their relationship is defined by the father's love and joy. The father did not require proof of change or evidence of repentance as a prerequisite to welcoming him back; he only required that the son return. The son did not allow his regret to keep him feeding pigs. His love for his father, his honesty in repentance restored him to his family. The father and son leave the mistakes and pain of the past and move forward into a fresh start.

God is not going to force you to love him or obey him. He may allow you to make stupid decisions that will not turn out the way you think they will, that will disappoint you, that might even break your heart…because he never stops watching the horizon, waiting for you to remember who he is, remember that you belong to him, and turn around to go home and find him waiting for you. No matter what you have done or what has been done to you, nothing will ever change the fact that you belong to him, that he loves you more than you can ask or imagine, and that he is always ready to forgive you and restore you into the fullness of relationship with him.

Why do we so often decide to punish ourselves in the "pigpens" that result from our stupid choices? What we deserve never matches what our Father feels for us. God never calls us to our "pigpens"; it does not honor him when we punish ourselves by staying in them. Regret can be a good thing if it moves you from where you were never intended to be, from where you no longer want to be – to where God is calling.

Your heavenly father is watching for you to leave where you never should have gone, to abandon the choices that have taken you away from him. He is not angry with you; he eagerly anticipates a fresh start. Don't let regret keep you away from "home". Trust that the father who loves you enough to give you the free will to leave loves you enough to welcome you back. Your confession doesn't have to be eloquent; he may not even let you finish. He knows your heart, and he is so focused on restoring relationship with you that he has everything ready to redeem you as his precious child.

Paul

Saul of Tarsus would have undoubtedly run away with the senior superlative of "most likely to succeed". The best recorded physical description of him comes from an apocryphal book *The Acts of Paul and Thecla* which dates at least back to the 2nd century. It describes him as short, bald, and bow legged, but he had advantages that added privilege and power to his intellect and passion for learning and prosecuting the law. He was from Tarsus, a city located on a trade route with a very diverse culture. He most likely would have spoken Greek in the marketplace, Aramaic at home, and Hebrew for his religious studies. His father was a tentmaker and was wealthy enough to afford the best tutor of that time. Gamaliel was the grandson of Hillel, one of the two men who defined the law and philosophy of the

Pharisees. Gamaliel's diatribe style of teaching, using question and answer style dialogue to lead students to right answers, is apparent in most of the New Testament epistles "Paul" will eventually write.

Saul's quick mind and incredible capacity for verbal expression allowed him to quickly rise to notoriety among the Pharisees. He became a lawyer for the Sanhedrin. His skill and understanding of the law of the Pharisees and his passion to persecute those who opposed that law gave him recognition among those he served, and generated fear among those he opposed. He also had the added advantage of Roman citizenship. He was protected by the Roman authorities. He even records his self-description of his early career.

Phil 3:4b-6 If anyone else thinks he has reasons to put confidence in the flesh, I have more: circumcised on the eighth day, of the people of Israel, of the tribe of Benjamin, a Hebrew of Hebrews; in regard to the law, a Pharisee; as for zeal, persecuting the church; as for legalistic righteousness, faultless.

In the eyes of the world he was admired, and he was well on his way to the top. He is first mentioned in scripture at the scene of Stephen's execution.

Acts 7:57-58 At this they covered their ears and, yelling at the top of their voices, they all rushed at him, dragged him out of the city and began to stone him. Meanwhile, the witnesses laid their clothes at the feet of a young man named Saul.

The Pharisees were undoubtedly frustrated that their execution of Jesus had not stopped the spread of Christianity. Saul did not have the half-hearted faith of Jews who incorporated God into their idolatry, who served God when it served their best interest and ignored God when it became inconvenient. He wholeheartedly submitted himself to the law. He believed that law was all that defined a relationship with God, and he vehemently opposed any heresy that might threaten the supremacy of that law.

Acts 26:9-11 I too was convinced that I ought to do all that was possible to oppose the name of Jesus of Nazareth. And that is just what I did in

Jerusalem. On the authority of the chief priests I put many of the saints in prison, and when they were put to death, I cast my vote against them. Many a time I went from one synagogue to another to have them punished, and I tried to force them to blaspheme. In my obsession against them, I even went to foreign cities to persecute them.

As Saul went to Damascus to carry out what he believed was the right course of action regarding the law, God interrupted his journey.

Acts 9:1-9 Meanwhile, Saul was still breathing out murderous threats against the Lord's disciples. He went to the high priest and asked him for letters to the synagogues in Damascus, so that if he found any there who belonged to the Way, whether men or women, he might take them as prisoners to Jerusalem. As he neared Damascus on his journey, suddenly a light from heaven flashed around him. He fell to the ground and heard a voice say to him, "Saul, Saul, why do you persecute me?" "Who are you, Lord?" Saul asked. "I am Jesus, whom you are persecuting," he replied. "Now get up and go into the city, and you will be told what you must do." The men traveling with Saul stood there speechless; they heard the sound but did not see anyone. Saul got up from the ground, but when he opened his eyes he could see nothing. So they led him by the hand into Damascus. For three days he was blind, and did not eat or drink anything.

It was sudden and personal. God called him by name and described Saul's behavior as an attack on God, rather than just punishment of his people. For the first time in Saul's life, he saw a God of relationship, rather than a God of laws. Heretofore, Saul's God was based on "head" information about a ritual, legalistic religion based on laws; suddenly, he was confronted by a relational, loving God. Jesus asked, "Why are you persecuting me?" Saul responded, "Who are you?" When Saul heard the answer "I am Jesus", he realized that all he had ever studied and all he had dedicated his life to was somewhere between completely wrong and woefully incomplete. The bright light caused him to be blind for three days, and he was led, helpless, into the city that he originally intended to take by storm.

He learned a hard truth; what he did with what he learned would forever change him and determine all that comes next. He could protect his power and reputation and ignore God; he could wallow in regret over the mistakes he had so passionately pursued, or he could move forward in an entirely new direction where he saw no real hope of success. He was told to walk away from his profession, his growing power base, and the beliefs he had built his life around to serve the one he had opposed. Saul the persecutor chose to become Paul the persecuted. His father, according to strict rabbinical law, would have disowned him for his conversion if he were still alive. Paul would be off the "A" list for party invitations with his Sanhedrin buddies back in Jerusalem. Jews saw him as a traitor; Christians saw him as a threat. He was probably more accepted by the Greeks that he used to disdain than the Jews that share his heritage. The only peace he would know from this point forward was the peace he would find in relationship with the one he formerly persecuted.

His assessment of his past is brutally honest. He doesn't sugar coat or attempt to excuse his past. He doesn't blame it on parents or his teachers. He accepts responsibility for what he's done and focuses on what needs to come next.

1 Tim 1:15 Here is a trustworthy saying that deserves full acceptance: Christ Jesus came into the world to save sinners--of whom I am the worst.

Many things about Paul remain unchanged after his conversion. His commitment to what he believed was just as zealous and selfless as it had always been, but suddenly he was committed to what he used to oppose. His passion was undiminished, but that passion was redirected to proclaiming Jesus, rather than persecuting those who trusted him. His ability to explain his beliefs was as eloquent and clear as his keen mind had always been, but his beliefs had changed.

What do you do when you realize that you've been wrong? That your passions and beliefs are flawed? That what you supported has let you down? That you have wasted time and effort and have only regret to show for it?

How deeply grateful I am for the honesty of God's word. He doesn't just give us the fairy tale, happily ever after version of the truth. He gives us the whole truth. Those who love him, who try desperately to do the right thing, will make bad choices with the best of intentions. We will come to a place where we learn that we were wrong, that our passion and beliefs may have been dedicated to unworthy ends. And it is with that painful perspective that we suddenly see that we worship a God who is not limited by our choices. This God can transform the mistakes of our past into the victory of our future. Saul's choices did not prevent God from using Paul. Nothing you have done is too big or too bad for God to redeem. But focusing on your regret can prevent God's redemption of your past from becoming victory in your future.

Paul didn't take his shame and regret and hide. God didn't meet him on the Damascus Road just to fuss at him. God's intention then and now when he interrupts the lives of those he loves is to change what they have been into what they can be. He wants what we've learned in the past to become a weapon we use to fight the very ignorance or evil that once held us captive.

Paul took what he learned about God in Hebrew school and from Gamaliel and became the most influential teacher and missionary of all time. He took all he had learned about God's law and wrote most of the New Testament. He spent the rest of his life sharing the passion and knowledge of his past in such a way that the future of Christianity took shape. His ability to explain and teach is still studied by Christians two thousand years later.

The innate sin of regret is that we decide that our mistakes are bigger than our God. We refuse to forgive others or ourselves and move past the problem. We believe that God may be able to forgive Paul or Moses or David, but what we have done or what has been done to us is just outside his capability to redeem. And there is the strategy Satan uses to keep us bound to the past and captive to our regret. From the Damascus Road forward, Paul is living proof that God can change any heart, can redeem any sin, and can create hope from nothing more than a contrite heart.

What you choose to take with you when you handle your regret absolutely matters. The Prodigal Son took the love of his family and went back home. Paul took his passion and his education all over the world. Both were permanently changed by the God who longs to forgive and create fresh starts whose foundations are often laid in the mistakes of the past. What we learn from those mistakes can become the weapons that give us victory in our future.

Chapter 8

People like you who felt shame or humiliation and struggle to move beyond what others think

A wise woman once told me that shame is Satan's thumbprint on our lives. Piper defines it as "a painful emotion caused by a consciousness of guilt or shortcoming or impropriety."[51] Satan will tempt us, hoping that we will not only sin, but that the shame from that sin will become a life sentence that we give to ourselves and accept from others. He can make us so focused on what we have done that we forget about God. Shame can make us decide that we are no better than our worst moment and incapable of accomplishing anything better, much less significant. If we allow it, shame will become the way we see ourselves. If we stay mired in the shame and guilt of our sin, we either won't repent or won't forgive ourselves because we decide the only thing that matters about us is our shame. Shame tells us that God may forgive our behavior, but somehow He is unable or unwilling to redeem us and restore relationship with him or hope for our future. Shame is not of God.

Shame can be public or private. It may be based on what you have or have not done. It can be the result of actions of those you associate with or something done to you. When you choose to associate yourself with that shame long enough, it becomes less about what was done, and more about who you are. Shame forces you to define yourself with your worst moments, and keeps your focus on yourself, not on God. Burton explains that the core tendency of shame is to move us from recognizing our sin to identifying ourselves with it. "Beyond doing something wrong, I am something wrong. I have something unacceptable to hide."[52]

What a difference a chapter makes. Before Adam and Eve sinned: "The man and his wife were both naked, and they felt no shame."(Gen 2:25) After they sinned: "Then the eyes of both of them were opened, and they realized they were naked; so they sewed fig leaves together and made coverings for themselves." (Gen 3:7) Notice that the shame was in the result of their sin, not actually the sin itself. What we do with our sin makes all the difference. How differently might the Bible have read if their first response to understanding the "knowledge of good and evil" was to seek God's presence and repent? But they didn't. They allowed their shame to control their response and concluded that fig leaves were their only option.

While not really the best choice for long lasting or comfortable clothing, fig leaves are large, and they were clearly handy in the garden. Can you imagine trying to wear leaves to protect your modesty? Have you seen what even the slightest breeze will do to leaves? Do you know how quickly leaves become brittle and fragile when they are not attached to the tree? Did they really think God wouldn't notice? Did they hope God would ignore their sin because they had such a snappy new outfit?

God was not fooled then, and he is not fooled now. Our attempts to hide our sin are as pathetic and obvious as their fig leaves were. And part of the problem with hiding anything is that it is not gone; we continue to live with the fear we will be exposed.

Hiding our sin will not remove the effects or consequences or punishment of our sin. Sin requires a blood sacrifice, and God had to kill animals to make clothes for them…to cover their sin and shame. But recognize that this was the first sin. Notice that the first "killing" in the Bible was at God's initiative to atone for their sin. God warned them that eating from the tree would bring death, and it did. (We don't know which animal was sacrificed to make their clothes, but it would be just like God for it to have been a lamb.)

Our choice to sin will bring us shame; how long we allow shame to control us is also our choice. The sources of our shame can be as varied as our appearance, our financial status, our behavior in a moment of weakness, the behavior of our family, or choices that we wish we could take back. God calls us to repentance, not to shame. There is nothing you have done that is greater than God's ability to forgive; there is nothing that has happened to you that is too severe for God to redeem.

Peter

I find great comfort in the character of Peter. He was never known for careful planning or introspection. He was impulsive and frequently let unfiltered words come out of his mouth. He impetuously jumped out of a boat to get to Jesus (at least twice!), and tried to protect his Lord by cutting off the ear of the servant of the High Priest. He is credited for the Great Confession and recognition that Jesus is the son of God, and he was one of the inner circle of disciples who received special instruction from Jesus during his ministry. And yet he is the one who denied even knowing Jesus.

Matt 26:31-35 Then Jesus told them, "This very night you will all fall away on account of me, for it is written: "'I will strike the shepherd, and the sheep of the flock will be scattered.' But after I have risen, I will go ahead of you into Galilee." Peter replied, "Even if all fall away on account of you, I never will." "I tell you the truth," Jesus answered, "this very night, before the rooster crows, you will disown me three times." But Peter declared, "Even if I have to die with you, I will never disown you." And all the other disciples said the same.

Peter wanted to believe that he was brave and unwavering in his devotion to Jesus. He wanted to believe that his commitment to the Christ was stronger than others who might falter when faced with fear. But Peter's confidence faded in the torchlight of those who came to arrest Jesus. His bravado disappeared as he watched the authorities lead his Lord away to be tried as a criminal.

Matt 26: 58, 69-75 But Peter followed him at a distance, right up to the courtyard of the high priest. He entered and sat down with the guards to see the outcome... Now Peter was sitting out in the courtyard, and a servant girl came to him. "You also were with Jesus of Galilee," she said. But he denied it before them all. "I don't know what you're talking about," he said. Then he went out to the gateway, where another girl saw him and said to the people there, "This fellow was with Jesus of Nazareth." He denied it again, with an oath: "I don't know the man!" After a little while, those standing there went up to Peter and said, "Surely you are one of them, for your accent gives you away." Then he began to call down curses on himself and he swore to them, "I don't know the man!" Immediately a rooster crowed. Then Peter remembered the word Jesus had spoken: "Before the rooster crows, you will disown me three times." And he went outside and wept bitterly.

Shame comes when what we want to believe about ourselves or what we want others to believe about us does not match the truth. Peter was forced to acknowledge that what he wanted to believe about himself and his love for Jesus was not true.

Notice that he followed Jesus...at a distance. He feared being associated with Jesus, but his curiosity would not let him hide. The Luke passage says that when the rooster crowed, Jesus turned and looked at Peter (Luke 22:61). In the middle of the mockery of his trial, Jesus was looking at Peter.

Can you imagine Peter's reaction when he heard that rooster crow? When he caught Jesus' eye? When he knew that Jesus knew? When he realized that the only time Jesus allowed those who despised him to control him, Peter, not only did not support Jesus, he had lied about even knowing him?

Denying that he knew Jesus three times was bad enough, but Peter had compounded the shame by making a big scene beforehand in front of the other disciples by announcing that no matter what, he would never deny his Lord. It is bad enough to face your limitations privately, but knowing that others know as well multiplies them exponentially. At the lowest, most difficult moment of Jesus' life, he knew that Peter denied him. With the events that would unfold that night, Peter believed he would never have the chance to make it right. Jesus would be dead before Peter could speak to him again.

There is no indication Peter was at the cross. Where did he go to weep those bitter tears? Explaining them to someone else would just expand his shame further. How did he spend that Sabbath? Did he go find his wife? The disciples? Did he admit his shame to them? Or did he hide it?

I would completely understand if Peter had just handed in his resignation as a disciple. He could go back home to be a fisherman again since he so clearly had failed at the most basic level as a disciple.

One of the most tender passages in all of scripture is in Mark 16. The women arrive at the tomb to find an angel there. This angel announces Jesus' resurrection and then gives them direction to "Go tell the disciples and Peter" that they will see Jesus again (vs 7). When the women deliver the message, John and Peter race to the tomb. (Luke 24:12) Later, Peter will jump out of a boat and swim/wade to the shore to get to the one that he denied knowing.

The next time we actually see Peter and Jesus talking is after the "cookout" on the beach. Jesus has prepared a charcoal fire on the beach where he's cooking fish for the disciples. The only other place in the New Testament that mentions a charcoal fire is in the courtyard of Jesus' trial where Peter warmed his hands.[53] I cannot imagine that the similarity was lost on Peter.

Scripture does not record Peter ever specifically discussing the denial with Jesus. Perhaps that was just between Peter and Jesus; perhaps it was never specifically discussed. But scripture does show Jesus countering Peter's three denials by asking three times "Simon, do you love me?" and then the three commands to "Feed my sheep". (John 21) Jesus didn't ask him to apologize three times; he asked him to declare his love three times. And then, perhaps the most merciful of all – he gave him a command. Jesus was not through with Peter because of his weakness or his shame; Jesus did not just make peace with Peter and then part ways; Jesus wanted him to leave the past in the past and move beyond it to obedience in the future.

Peter did not allow his shame to separate him from his Christ. He did not allow it to rob him of his relationship with God or diminish what God could accomplish through him in the future. Peter did not allow the shame of his sin to become another sin. His relationship with Christ was more important than his past.

Woman with the issue of blood

Lev 15:25 When a woman has a discharge of blood for many days at a time other than her monthly period or has a discharge that continues beyond her period, she will be unclean as long as she has the discharge, just as in the days of her period.

During biblical times, women were considered unclean during their menstrual cycle. Being "unclean", even through no sinful choice of their own, isolated the women during this part of the month. This passage in Leviticus 15 goes on to say that during her time of "uncleanness", anything she sits on or any bed she lies on are also unclean, and anyone who touches them or her is unclean as well. Until the ritual cleansing after this time of "uncleanness", she would not be able to enter the Temple courts to worship or light the candles for Sabbath or Feast days. These prohibitions would have been in addition to the physical problems of not being able to maintain a pregnancy in a culture that saw children as a sign of God's blessing.

Most scholars agree that the woman in this story had some sort of physical problem that caused this continuous bleeding for twelve years. Whether it was a hormonal imbalance or a more serious issue like cancer, she would almost certainly have been severely anemic, causing extreme fatigue, and she may have also suffered from insomnia, possibly headaches and leg cramps.

Mark 5:22-28 Then one of the synagogue rulers, named Jairus, came there. Seeing Jesus, he fell at his feet and pleaded earnestly with him, "My little daughter is dying. Please come and put your hands on her so that she will be healed and live." So Jesus went with him. A large crowd followed and pressed around him. And a woman was there who had been subject to bleeding for twelve years. She had suffered a great deal under the care of many doctors and had spent all she had, yet instead of getting better she grew worse. When she heard about Jesus, she came up behind him in the crowd and touched his cloak, because she thought, "If I just touch his clothes, I will be healed."

Her story is embedded in the middle of the story of the healing of Jairus' daughter. Jesus was on his way to heal the daughter of someone important, a daughter who mattered enough for her father to go find Jesus and kneel before him to "earnestly" plead for his help. Both women are physically suffering; neither is given a name. One is identified as belonging to her father, Jairus, a ruler of the synagogue, who comes to beg Jesus to touch and heal his daughter. The other is identified only by her uncleanness, her shame. No one was supposed to touch her. There is no indication that anyone made any effort to intercede for her; her shame isolated her.

We do not know how old this woman was. If she had ever had a husband, her uncleanness would have prevented any sexual relations between them and would have been legal justification for him to divorce her. (Deut 24:1) If she had never been married before this problem began, certainly this would have precluded any hope for marriage. She is alone.

This passage says that for twelve years she "suffered a great deal under the care of many doctors", spending everything she had...only to get worse. I do not even want to imagine what those doctors might have done to her. At best they were incapable; at worst they were charlatans who took advantage of a desperate woman. Their treatments may even have contributed to the continuous decline of her health.

She could have allowed her shame to grow into despair. No one would have blamed her for giving up. She could have allowed the unfairness of her situation to cause her to wallow in anger and resentment. But she didn't. She took her shame and her pain to Jesus.

As Jesus was on the way to heal someone else, she came up behind him. She did not ask for healing or even try to touch him. She is used to being shunned and outcast. For twelve years people have avoided her touch. Somehow, she had enough hope to reach out to touch his cloak.

How had she learned about Jesus? Why did she have even that shred of hope that his cloak may have just enough power to heal her? Had she seen him heal before? Travelled to Capernaum specifically to find him? Did she know that Jesus was the Son of God? If so, how? If she didn't know, why would she risk public humiliation and scorn of one who might fail like all the others who had taken her money? What in her character allowed her to continue to hope when she had been disappointed so many times before? What did she know about Jesus that led her try one more time?

Mark 5:29-34 Immediately her bleeding stopped and she felt in her body that she was freed from her suffering. At once Jesus realized that power had gone out from him. He turned around in the crowd and asked, "Who touched my clothes?" You see the people crowding against you," his disciples answered, "and yet you can ask, 'Who touched me?" But Jesus kept looking around to see who had done it. Then the woman, knowing what had happened to her, came and fell at his feet and, trembling with fear, told him the whole truth. He said to her, "Daughter, your faith has healed you. Go in peace and be freed from your suffering."

She came up behind him; she did not speak to him. She thought, she prayed, no one would notice. Hopefully, if she just touched his cloak, she would be healed and Jesus would not be defiled. But this was not an ordinary man. This was God made flesh. He was not defiled by her uncleanness; his holiness made her clean.

She wanted to sneak up and "touch and run", but his response to her shame was to call her out, to make the scene she wanted to avoid, to see her face to face because she mattered to him. Her culture may have defined her with the shame of her condition, and she may have accepted that shame. But Jesus did not see her, and does not see us, as defined by the shame of our past; he sees us as we can be. He did not see her as "unclean"; he called her "daughter", just like the daughter of Jairus he was going to heal. He gave credit to the woman's faith. He released her with peace, suddenly free from twelve years of physical suffering, emotional isolation and shame.

When I get to heaven, she is one that I will intentionally go and find. I want to hear the rest of her story. Did she follow him? Did she ever hear him preach again? Early church legend puts her on the road Jesus walked to Calvary. Did that really happen? Did she have friends and family to whom she could return, or did she start a brand new chapter in her life, free from shame, full of hope? This was not a "do-over"; she didn't get those twelve years back, but she does have a fresh start for a new life, completely different from the one she has led for the last twelve years. What did she do with the new start Jesus gave her?

Satan wants to rob us of our potential and our relationship with God, and shame is a very effective tool for that. When we measure ourselves by the world's standards, we may feel shame. When we allow ourselves to be defined by what is wrong, we continue to give it power over us. Sometimes our shame stems from our own choices. Sometimes it comes from the choices of those we love. Sometimes it comes from things over which we have no control at all. The world, and maybe even the people around us, judge us by a false standard and try to make us believe that our shame is the only important thing about us.

Part of the insidious consequence of shame is that we willingly give up our hope because we see only the overwhelming circumstances of our past and allow them to control our present. We cannot imagine how the mess we are in could ever be redeemed and made new. God sent his son to die and redeem us from our sins, but that redemption includes release from the shame that comes from sin as well. He never intended for us to be defined by shame; he redeemed us from that so that we can see ourselves through his eyes, a precious child restored to relationship with the Father because of his unconditional love.

When we turn the shame of what we have done into who we are, we believe the lies of Satan. Our choice to feel shame is a sentence we willingly place on ourselves when we refuse God's redemption. But when I choose to see myself as God sees me, I am more than the sins of my past; I am more than the poor choices I have made; I am greater than any evil that has been done to me. God sees me as his child.

There are so many ways that I do not measure up to the standard the world has decided is important. I do not match the world's definition of beautiful; I do not have enough money to buy all the things the world says I should have; my children are not perfect, and I do stupid things. But I am so much more than that to God. He sees my face in the crowd; he sees my shame, whatever its source, as something I need to leave in my past and move forward into a future I cannot even imagine.

One of the amazing things about God is that even our most shameful moments do not deter him from seeing us and loving us and giving us the peace we need to follow him to whatever is next for us. Jesus did not let the shame of Peter or the woman with the issue of blood separate him from them. At the tomb the angels told the women to "go tell the disciples and Peter". (Mark 16:7) In the chaos of the crowd, Jesus stopped to ask, "who touched me?" He sought out those who felt shame in order to heal them. Whatever its source, our "uncleanness" will be healed by his holiness.

What you do with your shame is your choice. You can hold on to your shame. You can carefully hide it away and revisit it often in your mind. You can nurture it until it becomes part of who you are…or you can take it to God. He will not be surprised or horrified by it; he already knows. What breaks his heart is that you bow to and honor your shame more than you honor him. You cling to your shame; he wants to rescue you from it.

The right thing to do with your sin and the shame that can result from it is to repent and trust God to redeem you.

I John 1:9 If we confess our sins, he is faithful and just and will forgive us our sins and purify us from all unrighteousness.

Once you have confessed your sin and repented from it, do not compound the consequences of that sin by hanging on to the shame of it. God's mercy and forgiveness is bigger than anything you have done. Christ died for all and his sacrifice covered the sin of all…you are no exception. Refusing to forgive yourself and let go of that sin means you think that God is insufficient. Here is what God says about our confessed sin:

Ps 103:11-12 For as high as the heavens are above the earth, so great is his love for those who fear him; as far as the east is from the west, so far has he removed our transgressions from us.

You cannot trust other people with your shame; you can trust God with it. Others may focus on your shame, and Satan may use that to cause them to sin with judgmentalism, hypocrisy, or pride. Nothing you have done is too big for God to redeem; nothing you face is too hard for him to fix and bring good from it, even if you cannot see a happy ending. He knows the truth about what you have done and what has been done to you, and he chooses to see you as you can be, not who you have been. God is not limited by your past, your reputation, your current circumstances, or your imagination. But your choice to define yourself with your shame may limit your ability to trust him and move forward. God does not just offer free healing if you can get to him; he wants relationship beginning right now, right where you are – even if you are covered in shame. God can forgive anything if you are willing to confess and repent. Once you receive his forgiveness, you may just need to forgive others or yourself and follow God to the next phase of your life. He can redeem what has been into what can be.

So what will you do with your shame? Will you allow that sin to define you, or will you base your self-worth on how God sees you? Shame can make us dress up in fig leaves and hide from God and each other, or it can drive us into the presence of the one whose holiness can make us clean. Choose to trust God's power to redeem you from the shame that Satan wants to use to keep you away from God's plan for the rest of your life.

Ps 34:5 Those who look to him are radiant; their faces are never covered with shame.

Now What?

Jesus warned us about the truth. "In this world you will have trouble." (John 16:33) People will mistreat you, disappoint you, and hurt you. You will make bad choices that have very real consequences. The power of evil and the frailty of your strength, wisdom, and best intentions can leave you fearful, desperate, and hopeless. Satan's goal for your life is that you believe his lies and trust your weakness so that he can separate you from the strength and love and power of God. Satan wants you to forfeit your peace and blessing by ensuring that you stay trapped in your past, and you never trust God enough to move forward. But Jesus' warning about the certainty of trouble was followed with the promise "Take heart! I have overcome the world."

There are hard days when it does not look like God is even paying attention to my world, much less has overcome all the things in it that threaten me or oppress me. There are things that I would much rather he protect me from than walk me through. But my assessment of "what things look like" does not include the things I cannot see and do not know. I can trust my limited perspective, or I can choose to have faith that he is who is says he is. I can choose to honor him as God, or I can pretend to be god for myself.

Whether or not we choose to obey God in the difficult, painful times indicates what we actually believe about God. Is He the God you cheerfully, willingly serve as long as you are getting your way? Do your circumstances change what you believe about God, or does what you believe about God change what you believe about your circumstances?

Our choices in those moments can separate us from God or make us open vessels that God can use to fill with his power. Burns writes that

"The revelation of God's faithfulness that transforms your character cannot happen without your willing cooperation."[54] When we obediently, faithfully handle the adversity and pain of our lives, God promises that he will "bestow on them a crown of beauty instead of ashes, the oil of gladness instead of mourning, and a garment of praise instead of a spirit of despair." (Is 61:3)

Each of us has an ash pile. Those ashes can be remnants of our plans and expectations. They may be all we have left after fear and pain have wounded our self-confidence and dreams. We can stir those ashes, hide the ashes, or simply protect the ashes, but nothing we do to them will ever make them anything more than ashes. God has promised to redeem the ashes of what has been and resurrect them into a crown of beauty. Your past is never too complicated or too far gone for God to redeem into something beautiful. Resurrection is God's specialty.

God has the power to spare us the pain of rejection or heartbreak or betrayal or shame. He can separate us from what makes us afraid or angry. But just because he can, does not mean he always will. Sometimes he allows the hard things into our lives. He may use those hard times to help us focus on him or to strengthen us or empower us to do more than we think we are capable of ever achieving. He may use our struggles to rescue another or serve as an example to those who are watching us. When we respond to those things by seeking God, we make room in our lives for his redemption to begin. When we respond to those things by separating ourselves from God, we sentence ourselves to struggling alone, trapped by the very things we so want to escape.

Our future is far less dependent on what has been than it is on our next answer to "Now What?". You have, more than likely, made enough bad choices to have confidence in your insecurity. You have real fear and failure and disappointment and regret and heartbreak and shame. Will you allow them to define you, or will you allow them to become your first step toward healing and strength? Will you accept defeat from the things and people who have stolen your joy and hope, or will you persevere until you have victory despite them? Will you allow your pain and your past to harden your heart and hold you captive, or will you allow God to mend the brokenness of your past in such a way that you are made stronger and more loving?

Of all the characters in the Bible, Job may be the best example of a man who had every right to wallow in the mess and pain of his life. Through no fault of his own he lost 7000 sheep, 3000 camels, 5000 oxen, 500 donkeys, many servants, all ten of his children, and his health. His friends told him his suffering was the result of his sin, and his wife told him to "Curse God and die." (Job 2:9) He knew incredible heartbreak and intense physical pain. Job trusted and obeyed God, and he suffered anyway. And then he did what we should all do...he took his pain and his fear and his disappointment with God to God.

Job was completely honest with God about his situation. He did not hold back his frustration or anger. He asked God why. God's response did not explain away Job's frustration or remove the pain of his past; God did not apologize for not protecting Job from all that had happened. He reminded Job that God is God and Job is not. God did not give Job understanding; he just helped Job begin again. And in so doing, God enabled Job to build a new future, despite the mess and pain of his past. Job's response:

Job 19:25 I know that my Redeemer lives.

Notice that Job does not describe God here as his Father or Provider or Healer or King. He does not appeal to God to fight for him as a mighty warrior or to avenge injustice as a judge. He claims God as his redeemer, one who will convert what was, what is, into something new.

The things that make us better and stronger are seldom things that we would choose. The only choice Job had, the only choice we have, is in our response to "Now What?". Burton says this about your response. "I'm convinced that on the other side of your difficult circumstances, something good is waiting, something better than you've previously thought or imagined. But to find it, you'll have to surrender your will and allow God's strength and grace to guide you."[55]

God does not intend for you to merely survive your past trials and be defined by your mistakes; God requires that you take responsibility for your mistakes, forgive others and yourself, and move on. He intends for you to use the hard, painful places in your life as a starting point for what is next. Tony Evans says that "God can't (or won't) change your past. But He can change your future, and that truth alone should give you hope."[56]

Sometimes God gives us understanding and closure to what has been; sometimes he just calls us forward despite what we do not understand. Whatever story and choices have brought you to where you are right now can be used by God to give you strength and wisdom for what is to come next.

There is a fascinating detail in the story of the Exodus that is often overlooked. At the burning bush, before Moses ever leaves the back side of the desert, God tells him that the Hebrews are to ask for plunder from the Egyptians as they leave.

Ex 3:22 Every woman is to ask her neighbor and any woman living in her house for articles of silver and gold and for clothing, which you will put on your sons and daughters. And so you will plunder the Egyptians.

What an incredibly odd command! God knows these people are about to begin a journey. They do not need extra "stuff" to carry around that is unnecessary for life in the desert. Why would God tell them to bring along what they do not need? Wouldn't it have been smarter for them to stock up on food and water? Maybe an extra pair of sandals? Medicine or herbs?

The odd thing about making a new start that we have to choose what plunder we take with us from our past. Your past struggles and choices may have you laden with pain or anger or brokenness that you haul around, that weighs you down, that you certainly do not need and that prevents you from fully embracing the fresh start you so desire. God desires that the plunder we take from where we have been help us grow and become more holy in the fresh start he so desires for us. Twenty-two chapters after that odd command, God's plan starts to come into focus.

Ex 25:1-8 The LORD said to Moses, "Tell the Israelites to bring me an offering. You are to receive the offering for me from each man whose heart prompts him to give. These are the offerings you are to receive from them: gold, silver and bronze; blue, purple and scarlet yarn and fine linen; goat hair; ram skins dyed red and hides of sea cows; acacia wood; olive oil for the light; spices for the anointing oil and for the fragrant incense; and onyx stones and other gems to be mounted on the ephod and breastpiece. Then have them make a sanctuary for me, and I will dwell among them."

They are in the middle of a desert. None of the things on this "offering list" would have been available in the wilderness; nor would they be things they would have logically chosen to take with them because they knew they would need them for the journey. God met all their needs during the forty years between their slavery in Egypt and their beginning to reclaim their promised land. Their shoes and clothes did not wear out. (Ex 29:5) He miraculously fed them with manna and quail and brought water from a rock to quench their thirst. God healed their diseases and protected them from their enemies. What God asked from them was the plunder of where they had been so they could build a sanctuary where he could meet with them. God provided what they would need to survive; he asked them to bring what would allow them to worship.

What you bring from your past matters as you meet God in your present. What plunder have you carried away from your past? Guilt? Anger? Wisdom? Compassion? Has the plunder from your past made you better, stronger, more loving, more powerful? Or has it made you more timid, less trusting, more selfish, less hopeful, more afraid? God never intends our struggles to be for nothing or leave us weaker. He intends that our struggles prepare us for victory in our future.

Sometimes our fresh start begins with intentionally setting aside what we should never have carried this long. Sometimes it means giving to God what will allow him to meet us where we are. Sometimes it requires that we leave where we never should have gone and return to him. It always requires that we forgive others or ourselves and let the past be the past and no longer control our present or shape our future. We can choose to be controlled by our bad choices, or we can return to our father. We can be captive to what we have done, or we can do something new. When we choose to trust God with the details of our journey forward and take only what will allow us to be in his presence, we will find him in the midst of the desert that will lead us to our Promised Land.

Their plunder, and ours, was not for them; it was for God. Their plunder became the tabernacle where God would dwell among them. Our plunder can become the strength and passion for spiritual growth and ministry. Hanging on to our pain and problems can keep us trapped in them; realizing that we worship the God who can redeem our past will not only give us victory over it, but also courage for what is to come.

God specializes in fresh starts. Anyone can throw away what is damaged; only God can redeem us and give us new hope.

II Cor 5:17 Therefore, if anyone is in Christ, he is a new creation; the old has gone, the new has come!

Ez 18:31 Rid yourselves of all the offenses you have committed, and get a new heart and a new spirit.

Is 43:19 See, I am doing a new thing! Now it springs up; do you not perceive it? I am making a way in the desert and streams in the wasteland.

Your desert may be the consequences of your bad choices in the "far country"; your wasteland may be what lost opportunities have done to your present circumstances. Leave your past in the past; refuse to allow it to define you anymore. Give the plunder God commands that you take from lessons learned the hard way to him, and let him refocus your energy and give you hope for the new thing he wants to do for you and in you. Meet him for a fresh start in your present as he prepares you for the Promised Land he has prepared for you, both here on earth and in eternity.

God led his people away from Egypt, where they were enslaved, to Palestine, where they would be at home, and the journey between the two absolutely mattered. When the Hebrews were trapped between the Red Sea and the Egyptian army, they could not see any hope of rescue. But God was not bound by what they could see or even predict; God opened a way through the sea, and they passed through it on dry ground. (Ex 14:16) God did not offer them several options for their escape route and allow them to choose. God did not make the Egyptian army disappear. The Hebrews did not fly over the Red Sea or go around it; they passed through it...on the way to their Promised Land. And when they got to the Promised Land they passed through the Jordan River on dry land as well.

They had to make that journey....step by step, day by day, year by year....until they reached home. From the parting of the Red Sea until stopping the flow of the Jordan, God went before them and made a way for them. That journey provided ample opportunities for them to know fear of very powerful enemies. Some even regretted leaving Egypt. During their time in the wilderness they celebrated births and grieved deaths. They knew sickness and hunger and thirst. They were disappointed in everything from the menu to the length of time it took to get home. They betrayed God by worshipping a golden calf. They depended on God and Moses to take care of them because they were incapable of taking care of themselves. But God never abandoned them. He never let their poor choices separate them from him. He never abandoned those who ignored him. Their journey home was fraught with disobedience and difficulty and inconvenience and pain, but God led them away from their captors and into the Promised Land on dry ground. Everything they faced on the journey home made arriving in their Promised Land more precious.

We are no different. God does not just magically teleport us to heaven when we decide to follow him. We have to face this life one step at a time, one day at a time, year after year. We will pass through hard times and painful places. We will make bad choices that cause us to suffer, and we will suffer because of the sinful choices of those around us. Too often we learn the hard way that God's way is best. This world will bring us pain and regret, insecurity, fear and disappointment. We will face enemies and obstacles that are bigger than we can defeat alone...and we don't have to. God goes before us, each step, each day, preparing the way. Sometimes He grows our faith by guiding us when we cannot see the way or the plan. Sometimes He gives us rest and comfort when we are overwhelmed. Always He leads us toward home. When we follow Him, He will make a way for us. When life seems like it will drown us or sweep us away, when we feel stuck in the mire of our circumstances, God can lead us forward on dry ground.

What happened to Job wasn't fair; neither was the enslavement of the Hebrews. When I'm trying so hard to do the right thing and I get hurt anyway, that isn't fair either. Life has not been "fair" since the serpent showed up in Eden. The presence of sin and evil in this world automatically makes life unfair. It was human choice that made us responsible for our knowledge of good and evil, and now we must decide what we will chose for what is to come. Batterson summarizes the problem like this: "One of our fundamental spiritual problems is this: we want God to do something new while we keep doing the same old thing."[57] Defending our past choices and behavior will not improve our future outcomes. Focusing on what others have done to us will not change us for the better. Our response to "now what?" needs to begin with confession and repentance, followed by daily obedience to one who already knows what is next.

Even if you believe that "fairness" will work itself out as justice in Judgment and eternity, that belief will offer little comfort now. Barbara Brown Taylor reminds us: "We cannot control everything that happens to us. That is the human condition, and it can be frightening, because what that means is that we cannot choose all the circumstances of our lives. All we can really choose is how we respond to them..."[58]

What you and I will face during our time on earth will be hard. God may not make those things go away. He may not give us the option of going around them; he may choose to walk us through them. And when he does, our safety and hope and redemption depends on whether or not we follow him to the other side.

II Cor 4:8-9 We are hard pressed on every side, but not crushed; perplexed, but not in despair; persecuted, but not abandoned; struck down, but not destroyed.

Paul admonishes the Romans to be "patient in affliction". (Rom 12:12) However deep or painful the wounds of your affliction may be, whether those afflictions are self-inflicted, undeserved, or well deserved, God can rescue you and redeem you. He can strengthen you and deal righteously with those who wounded you. He is not limited by what you are; he sees you as you can be. And when you focus on God's vision of your potential and future, you can leave behind the hindrances that keep you from moving forward.

Getting "caught" in Satan's schemes and snares may or may not be an accident, but staying captive is your choice. How you handle your past is the best indication of what you believe about God. The only power your past has over you is the power you choose to give it to control your future. When you allow God to repair your past, he uses it to prepare you for what is to come. Beth Moore says:

> "Every time we've been broken and then allowed God to repair us, that mending becomes part of our equipping. All the pain we've endured. All the abuse and misuse. Every betrayal. Every wound. Where God mends, He equips... If we still have life and breath, God can repurpose every shred of havoc the Devil wreaks."[59]

The big names of the Bible had nothing in common except that they obeyed God by refusing to be bound by their afflictions. They believed that "Sometimes when things are falling apart, they may actually be falling into place."[60] They were ordinary people, just like you and me, who chose to trust God to make what "had been" into what "could be".

Will you trust God to be who he says he is, or will you continue to do what you've been doing, hoping for different results? He is God; you are not. Refuse to continue to be weighed down by the things in your life that you cannot change. Rather than pretending to be in charge, trust the one who is. Rather than being defined by what you believe you cannot do, trust the one who can do anything. Rather than hiding being your fear, trust the one who has all power and authority. Rather than withdrawing or being angry when God's plan does not line up with your plan, trust the one who knows the future. Rather than allowing unforgiveness to harden your heart, trust the one who perfectly merges justice and mercy to handle those who have hurt you. Rather than hanging on to the pain of loss and heartbreak, trust the one who can heal and make all things new. Rather than defining yourself by your past mistakes, trust the one who wants to give you a fresh start. Rather than defining yourself by what others think, trust the one who loved you enough to die for you so that your eternity will be spent with him.

Heb 12:1 **Therefore, since we are surrounded by such a great cloud of witnesses, let us throw off everything that hinders and the sin that so easily entangles, and let us run with perseverance the race marked out for us.**

Sometimes your "race", your journey home, is on even ground with a pleasant view; most of the time it is not. There are often obstacles in your path that can cause you to stumble or stop altogether. How you respond to those obstacles determines the course of your life. Runners train themselves to clear the hurdles on their path. It would be ridiculous for a runner to pick up and carry the hurdles as he runs. His focus should be on the finish line, not the hurdles. His ability to finish and win the race depends on his clearing the hurdles, not collecting them. Hurdles do not belong at the finish line. Yet so many of us insist on carrying our insecurity, our fears, our disappointments, our unforgiveness, our pain, our shame, and our past into the future where they no longer belong. We serve and carry what weighs us down and holds us back because our focus is on the obstacle, not the finish line.

Sometimes our suffering is the result of our own choices; sometimes it results from situations over which we have not control. But either way, we cannot change what has been; we can only change what will be. If we do not choose to let go of our excuses and the sources of our pain, we will eventually die, still clutching that pain. Or we can leave the past in God's hands and live our life, free to experience and handle all that is to come.

Your response to the tests and trials of your life becomes your testimony. Your life has "witnesses" that are encouraging you to throw off your hindrances and other witnesses that may follow your example. God had you in his heart when he recorded the stories of the Bible. He knew you would need them. The big stories, the famous moments of the Bible focus on people who chose God, no matter what. Their faith is our example. They were ordinary people like you and me who obeyed and trusted an extraordinary God. God preserved their stories to give us hope…because as long as we are alive, he wants us to move forward. May we have the courage to dare to ask God to help us focus on what can be, rather than what has been. May he give us a passion to become all that he created us to be, and may we never limit his power or our potential by remaining trapped by things that diminish us. May we follow the good example of biblical people just like us and know the power and presence of Almighty God who can redeem all that has been into more than we can ask or imagine.

Endnotes

Introduction

[1]   Numerous sources attribute this quote to Thomas Edison, but I was unable to specifically document it from any primary source.

[2]   Jud Wilhite. *Pursued.* New York: Faith Words, 2013, p. 9.

[3]   Wayne Barber, Eddie Rasnake, and Richard Shepherd. *Following God: Life Principles from the Prophets of the Old Testament.* Chatanooga: AMG Publishers, 1999, p. 56.

Chapter 1

[4]   Terry Powell. *Serve Strong.* Leafwood Publishers, 2014, p. 105.

[5]   Charles Stanley. *Landmines in the path of the Believer.* Nashville: Thomas Nelson, 2007, p. 25.

[6]   http://www.ancient.eu/nineveh

[7]   Albert Kirk Grayson. *Assyrian Royal Inscriptions, Part 2: From Tiglath-pileser I to Ashur-nasir-apli II.* Wiesbaden, Germany: Otto Harrassowitz, 1976, p. 126.

[8]   Barber p. 55.

[9]   Norman Blackaby and Gene Wilkes. *Character: The Pulse of a Disciple's Heart.* Birmingham, Al: New Hope Publishers, 2012, p.71.

[10]   Tony Evans. *It's Not Too Late.* Nashville: Lifeway Press, 2012, p. 89.

[11]   Barbara Brown Taylor. *The Preaching Life.* Cambridge, MA: Cowley Publications, 1993, p. 131.

[12]   ngie Smith. *What Women Fear.* Nashville, B&H Publishing Group, 2011, p. 139-140.

Chapter 2

[13]   Lisa TerKeurst. *What Happens When Women Say Yes to God.* Eugene, Or: Harvest House Publishers, 2007, p. 95.

14   Beth Moore. *So Long Insecurity.* Carol Stream, Ill: Tyndale House Publishers, Inc. 2007, p. 326-328.
15   Kelly Minter. *Nehemiah.* Nashville: Lifeway Press, 2012, p. 53.
16   Ronald E. Youngblood. *Nelson's New Illustrated Bible Dictionary.* Nashville: Thomas Nelson Publishers, 1995, p. 1126.
17   *Ibid,* p. 835.
18   Priscilla Shirer. *Gideon.* Nashville: Lifeway Press, 2013, p. 107.
19   Mark Batterson. *All In.* Grand Rapids, MI: Zondervan, 2013, p. 107.
20   *Ibid,* p. 109.

Chapter 3

21   Burton, Valorie. *Where Will You Go from Here?* Colorado Springs: Waterbook Press, 2011, p. 65.
22   David Jeremiah. *What Are You Afraid Of?* Carol Stream, IL: Tyndale House Publishers, 2013, p. ix.
23   Biblestudytools.com
24   Jeremiah, p. xiv.
25   *Ibid,* p. xiv.
26   http://animals.about.com/od/Snakes/p/vipers.htm
27   http://www.biblearchaeology.org
28   John Piper. *Future Grace.* Colorado Springs: Multnomah Books, 2012, p. 51.
29   John MacArthur. *Twelve Unlikely Heroes.* Nashville: Thomas Nelson, 2012, p. 41.
30   Jennie Allen. *Chase.* Nashville: Thomas Nelson Publisher, 2012, p. 53.

Chapter 4

31   Stanley, p. 143.
32   Philip Yancey. *Disappointment with God.* Zondervan: Grand Rapids, MI, 1988, p. 41.
33   MacArthur, p. 161.
34   *Ibid,* p. 158.
35   *Ibid,* p. 167.
36   Mark Batterson. *All In,* p. 87.
37   Mark Batterson. *The Circle Maker.* Grand Rapids, MI, Zondervan, 2011, p. 113.
38   Taylor, p. 10.
39   Sheila Walsh. *The Storm Inside.* Nashville: Nelson Books, 2014, p. 39.

Chapter 5

[40] Tim Burns. *Forged in the Fire: Shaped by the Master.* Tulsa, OK: Hensley Publishing, 2003, p. 129.

[41] Charles, R. Swindoll. *Joseph.* Nashville: Word Publishing, 1998, p. 55.

[42] MacArthur, p. 41.

Chapter 6

[43] http://personalitycafe.com/general-psychology/5995-emotional-health-understanding-our-primary-secondary-emotions.html

Chapter 7

[44] Kyle Idleman. *AHA: The God Moment That Changes Everything.* Colorado Springs: David C. Cook, 2014, p. 53.

[45] *Ibid*, p. 19.

[46] *Ibid*, p. 16.

[47] *Ibid*, p. 20.

[48] www.bibarch.com/archaeologicalsites/Decapolis.htm

[49] Idleman, p. 48.

[50] *Ibid*, p. 49.

Chapter 8

[51] Piper, p. 127.

[52] Burton, p. 65.

[53] Evans, *It's Not Too Late.* p. 126.

Conclusion

[54] Burns, p. 120.

[55] Burton, p. 5.

[56] Tony Evans. *God's Unlikely Path to Success.* Eugene, Or: Harvest House Publishers, 2012, p. 14.

[57] Batterson, <u>All In</u>, p. 55.

[58] Taylor, p. 97.

[59] Beth Moore. *Children of the Day.* Nashville: Lifeway Press, 2014, p. 159.

[60] Very Jane on face book.

Bibliography

Allen, Jennie. Chase. Nashville: Thomas Nelson Publisher, 2012.

Barber, Wayne, Eddie Rasnake, and Richard Shepherd. Following God: Life Principles from the Prophets of the Old Testament. Chatanooga: AMG Publishers, 1999.

Batterson, Mark. All In. Grand Rapids, MI: Zondervan, 2013.

Batterson, Mark. The Circle Maker. Grand Rapids, MI, Zondervan, 2011.

Blackaby, Norman and Gene Wilkes. Character: The Pulse of a Disciple's Heart. Birmingham, Al: New Hope Publishers, 2012.

Burns, Tim. Forged in the Fire: Shaped by the Master. Tulsa, OK: Hensley Publishing, 2003.

Burton, Valorie. Where Will You Go from Here? Colorado Springs: Waterbook Press, 2011.

Evans, Tony. God's Unlikely Path to Success. Eugene, Or: Harvest House Publishers, 2012.

Evans, Tony. It's Not Too Late. Nashville: Lifeway Press, 2012.

Grayson, Albert Kirk. Assyrian Royal Inscriptions, Part 2: From Tiglath-pileser I to Ashur-nasir-apli II. Wiesbaden, Germ.: Otto Harrassowitz, 1976

Idleman, Kyle. AHA: The God Moment That Changes Everything. Colorado Springs: David C. Cook, 2014.

Jeremiah, David. What Are You Afraid Of? Carol Stream, IL: Tyndale House Publishers, 2013.

MacArthur, John. Twelve Unlikely Heroes. Nashville: Thomas Nelson, 2012.

Minter, Kelly. Nehemiah. Nashville: Lifeway Press, 2012.

Moore, Beth. So Long Insecurity. Carol Stream, Ill: Tyndale House Publishers, Inc. 2007.

Moore, Beth. Children of the Day. Nashville: Lifeway Press, 2014.

Piper, John. Future Grace. Colorado Springs: Multnomah Books, 2012.

Powell, Terry. Serve Strong. Leafwood Publishers, 2014.

Shirer, Priscilla. Gideon. Nashville: Lifeway Press, 2013.

Smith, Angie. What Women Fear. Nashville, B&H Publishing Group, 2011.

Stanley, Charles. Landmines in the path of the Believer. Nashville: Thomas Nelson, 2007.

Swindoll, Charles R. Joseph. Nashville: Word Publishing, 1998.

Taylor, Barbara Brown. The Preaching Life. Cambridge, MA: Cowley Publications, 1993

TerKeurst, Lysa. What Happens When Women Say Yes to God. Eugene, Or: Harvest House Publishers, 2007.

Walsh, Sheila. The Storm Inside. Nashville: Nelson Books, 2014.

Wilhite, Jud. Pursued. New York: Faith Words, 2013.

Yancey, Philip. Disappointment with God. Zondervan: Grand Rapids, MI, 1988.

Youngblood, Ronald E. Nelson's New Illustrated Bible Dictionary. Nashville: Thomas Nelson Publishers, 1995.

http://www.ancient.eu/nineveh/

http://animals.about.com/od/Snakes/p/vipers.htm

www.bibarch.com/archaeologicalsites/Decapolis.htm

www.biblestudytools.com

http://personalitycafe.com/general-psychology/5995-emotional-health-understanding-our-primary-secondary-emotions.html

Very Jane/Facebook

Discussion Guide for
God Chooses People Like You

One thing I have learned from teaching Bible studies: deep learning and long term commitment to a group requires a perfect blend of godly information and safe, sweet fellowship among the participants. This study guide is intended to help you lead your group in discussion and analysis after they've read the corresponding chapters in the book *God Chooses People Like You*. The content of this book requires examination of some topics that may be very painful for the members of your group. As you prepare for each session:

1. Recognize the power of your prayers for each member of your group – both before the group begins to meet and during the study.
2. Remind them that things shared in this group are confidential unless specific permission is given to share.
3. Encourage each person to participate and try to discourage them from solving each other's problems during group discussion… this will hopefully lead each individual to God; it is not intended to be a group therapy session.
4. Use this discussion guide as a starting place, not as the final product. It is only one tool to help you lead your group. Feel free to add and make changes that would benefit the strengths and needs of your particular group.
5. Some of the discussion questions may require very personal answers. Use your own discretion as to whether or not to discuss these as a group or use them in a time of guided silent prayer.

Know that I am committed to praying for the open hearts and minds of the leaders and participants who will read the book and who will seek God as a result. May your study of the character of God cause you to humbly bow down and go confidently into his presence.

Please share your stories with me on my blog at **beverlycarrollrva@ wordpress.com** or by email at **beverlycarrollrva@gmail.com.**

Introduction

1. What do you know to be true about the world we live in today?
2. What do you know is true about you?
3. What do you know is true about God?
4. What are some reasons why the people in the Bible and we choose to disobey God or alter what he asks us to do into something less than full obedience, something we are more comfortable with? How is "partial obedience" disobedience?
5. Other than God, Jesus, and the Holy Spirit, Name the ten most important people in the Bible. What do they have in common? (You may want to divide them into groups and compare lists.)
6. How are they different from you?
7. Which was the most important thing about them: their capability or their choices? Why?
8. What is the difference between a Savior and a Lord?
9. Why did God preserve all those stories in the Bible? Why not just his laws and Jesus' sermons? Why not just make it a how to book?
10. What choices have you made that have kept you from knowing God's presence? That have prevented his power from manifesting itself in your life?

Chapter 1
People like you who don't like what God called them to do and struggle with pride

1. Why would the God who loves us want us to do something we don't like?
2. In the book of Jonah the word "appointed" (provided) is used 4 times (fish, vine, worm, wind). How does God use things that make us unhappy for our good?
3. Who are some people that "hate" each other in our time?
4. Where does the line between hatred of evil and acknowledgment of God's mercy lie?

5. Eph 4:26 "In your anger, do not sin." Where is the line between anger and sin?

6. When has God shown you the kind of grace that allows you start over?

7. Who needs that kind of grace from you?

8. What is your "one thing" that separates you from God's call on your life?

9. What are some things that we tend to be proud of? What problems can pride create?

10. How are delayed obedience and partial obedience – disobedience?

11. What do Jonah and the Rich Young Ruler have in common?

12. Why would we argue with or ignore God if we believe he is who he says he is?

Chapter 2
People like you who aren't qualified to do what God calls them to do and struggle with insecurity

1. What's the difference between the image you create of yourself and who you really are?

2. How do you develop confidence?

3. What are you qualified to do?

4. Why might your confidence be an impediment to God's working in your life?

5. What truth about yourself are you most afraid of? To be wrong? To be alone? To fail? Why?

6. What is the difference between what Nehemiah is good at, what he is trained to do, and what God calls him to do?

7. What is the difference between a task and a goal?

8. What walls do you need to build so that God can begin something new in your life? What in your life needs protection from outside threat? What do you need to separate yourself from in order to begin something new with God?

9. Why doesn't God always reward obedience with "happily ever after"?

10. Gideon had to tear down the Asherah pole before God would use him to lead his people. What do you need to "tear down" to make sure you serve only one God?

11. Compare/Contrast the tests Gideon gives God and the tests God gives Gideon.

12. How much time do you spend in prayer asking God to show you and equip you for what is next? Why is that significant?

Chapter 3

People like you who were afraid of what God called them to do and struggle with fear

1. What are some things you fear?

2. What do you do when you're afraid?

3. What are some times in the Bible when God's people were afraid?

4. What do you know about God that should impact your response to what you fear?

5. What does it mean to fear God? Why is it proper for us to fear God?

6. What are your strengths? Why would God ever ask you to do something that is not one of your strengths?

7. Why would God ask for obedience if we're afraid?

8. How did Moses' fear come from his weakness? How did Joshua's fear came from his strength?

9. Discuss the symbolism of the staff and the sword.

10. One of the promises God makes in the Bible is that "You will have trouble in this world." (John 16:33) Why do we try so hard to avoid the inevitable? Do you believe that "he has overcome the world"?

11. What evidence do you see of Satan's power? What evidence do you see that God has power over Satan?

Chapter 4

People like you who are disappointed in God and struggle to obey God when God doesn't obey them

1. Think back to a time that you were disappointed. What causes disappointment?
2. Why would God ever say "wait" to a godly request? Why would he ever say "no"?
3. Why did Jesus weep at the tomb?
4. How did this event change Martha and Mary's understanding of God?
5. What's the difference between what would have happened if Jesus had honored what they wanted, and what actually happened?
6. How can you tell the difference between God's "wait" answer to your prayers, and a "no" answer?
7. How can disappointment cause you to sin?
8. How did John, Martha, and Mary handle their disappointment well?
9. What is the difference between knowledge and belief? What prevents knowledge from becoming belief?
10. What do you know about God from his activity in your past that allows you to trust him for good in your present?
11. Ask for some to share stories of what started as their own disappointments, but turned out to be God's blessings.
12. Ps 37:4 Delight yourself in me and I will give you the desires of your heart. What keeps us from knowing delight? Why is delight so common in children and so rare in adults? When is the last time God delighted you?

Chapter 5

People like you who were betrayed by people they love and struggle with unforgiveness

1. What did Joseph learn in slavery, Potiphar's house and jail that prepared him for what was to come? Can you look back at something in your life that seemed horrible at the time that you now recognize was essential for your good?
2. How is sin like slavery? How is it like prostitution?
3. How can someone betray you? What does betrayal look like in real life?
4. For what reasons would someone choose to betray someone else?
5. How is betrayal different from your run of the mill lies or bullying?
6. What does a vengeful attitude indicate about your view of God?
7. "God was with Joseph". This was rare in the Old Testament and common after Pentecost. We now have unlimited access to power and presence of God. Why don't we access it more often?
8. Why is it important to forgive people who are not sorry? What impact does our unforgiveness have on us? On our testimony? On the ones we chose not to forgive?
9. Hos 2:14-16 What is the difference between a husband and a master?
10. What is the difference between forgiveness and restoration?
11. How can being betrayed cause us to sin?
12. When have you betrayed God?

Chapter 6

People like you who were heartbroken and struggle to let go of their pain

1. What is the difference between disappointment and heartbreak?
2. What are typical responses or behaviors associated with a broken heart?
3. Why does heartbreak so often cause us to doubt God or diminish our faith?

4. How is Mary Magdalen's response to Jesus' death different from everyone else's?

5. How would you characterize Thomas' relationship with Jesus before the Crucifixion?

6. How is Thomas' response to Jesus' death different from the other disciples' response?

7. How can a broken heart trap us in the past and prevent us from moving forward?

8. How do you see that brokenness can lead to new life? To better understanding and more compassion?

9. How has your heartbreak in the past strengthened you?

10. Why would the story of these two responses to Jesus' death be told in scripture, when the stories of the others were not told? What are we to learn from them?

11. Which faith is greater, that which never doubts, or that which investigates doubt and is satisfied? Why?

12. *"Blessed are those who have not seen and yet believe."* Why does the faith of those who have not seen receive a greater blessing?

Chapter 7

People like you who have regret and struggle to let go of their past

1. What causes regret?

2. How does regret cause you to doubt yourself?

3. How can regret tempt you to disobey God?

4. How do we serve things that are unclean?

5. If the father of the Prodigal is Jesus' explanation of how God loves us, how does God view your regrets?

6. How is Paul's conversion different from all the others in the Bible?

7. What about Paul did NOT change after his conversion?

8. What did change after his conversion?

9. With all Paul survived and accomplished, why would he characterize himself as the chief among sinners?

10. What's the difference between doing things for God, and allowing God to work through you?
11. Why would God allow Paul to be persecuted for obedience?
12. What's the difference between being spiritual and religious? Between being either of those and being a Christian?

Chapter 8
People like you who felt shame or humiliation and struggle to move beyond what others think

1. What is the difference between doing something wrong and being something wrong?
2. Where is the line between recognizing sin as sin, and choosing to be defined by our sin?
3. What kinds of things do we hide?
4. Why do we "hide" things?
5. How do we "hide" things?
6. How did God respond to Adam and Eve's effort to hide their sin?
7. How did Peter respond to his shame?
8. How did the woman respond to her shame?
9. Is there anything in your past that is still painful? Why is it still painful?
10. When have the opinions of others affected your opinion of yourself?
11. How have the opinions of others affected your willingness to trust God?
12. How can shame cause us to sin?

Conclusion

1. What do you need to let go of to move forward and deeper in your relationship with God?
2. Why let them go if the person who caused them isn't sorry or if you are still suffering because of them?
3. How have you been guilty of wounding another in the same way you've been wounded?
4. What keeps you from obeying God?
5. What power have you given to those who dislike you or want to destroy you?
6. Why are we far less likely to grow spiritually, to see more of God's character or plan, when things are going like we want them to?
7. How do you build a new future or life on old foundations that are scarred by your past?
8. How do you learn to trust your Ebeneezers, rather than your present circumstances or your past failures?

CPSIA information can be obtained at www.ICGtesting.com
Printed in the USA
BVOW08s0743121015

421861BV00002B/2/P

9 781512 708400